The
Divine Order
of the End Times

CLAYTON CARPENTER

WWW.BRIGHTSWORDCRUSADES.COM

WESTBOW
PRESS®
A DIVISION OF THOMAS NELSON
& ZONDERVAN

WestBow Press books may be ordered through booksellers or by contacting:

WestBow Press
A Division of Thomas Nelson & Zondervan
1663 Liberty Drive
Bloomington, IN 47403
www.westbowpress.com
1 (866) 928-1240

Scripture taken from the King James Version of the Bible.

Scripture taken from the New King James Version®. Copyright © 1982 by Thomas Nelson. Used by permission. All rights reserved.

Scripture taken from the Amplified Bible, copyright © 1954, 1958, 1962, 1964, 1965, 1987 by The Lockman Foundation. Used by permission.

ISBN: 978-1-5127-7919-6 (sc)
ISBN: 978-1-5127-7920-2 (hc)
ISBN: 978-1-5127-7918-9 (e)

Library of Congress Control Number: 2017903590

Print information available on the last page.

WestBow Press rev. date: 3/6/2017

Contents

CHAPTER 1

⊷⫯⊷ ⫯⊷

The Coming of the Lord and What to Look For

2 Thessalonians 2:1–12

The Restraining

I want to start by asking you the same questions that came to my mind and changed my thinking about eschatology (the study of the end times) and the direction for my study of the subject. Please look at 2 Thessalonians with me. "And now ye know what withholdeth that he might be revealed in his time. For the mystery of iniquity doth already work: only he who now letteth will let, until he be taken out of the way. And then shall that Wicked be revealed" (2 Thessalonians 2:6–8).

Lawlessness is at work, and its eyes are set on dominating humankind. Only there is something that is restraining this lawlessness from overwhelming the earth. Obviously, whoever or whatever is restraining this lawlessness is keeping the lawless one (the Antichrist) from being revealed. Now I have heard that (1) it is the Holy Spirit that is restraining the lawless one and that as soon as the Holy Spirit is taken out of the earth, then the lawless one will be able to take power. I've also heard that (2) this verse is speaking of the church—Christians—and that as soon as the rapture occurs and we're gone, then the lawless one will be able to take power.

I now wish to discuss what is restraining this lawlessness.

1

Clayton Carpenter

The Holy Spirit Is Restraining Lawlessness

First, what I have to say about the Holy Spirit restraining this lawlessness is as follows: If the Holy Spirit is taken out of the earth, then how will anyone be saved?

In Revelation 14, we're told that the gospel will be preached during the time of the Antichrist.

> And I saw another angel fly in the midst of heaven, having the everlasting gospel to preach unto them that dwell on the earth, and to every nation, and kindred, and tongue, and people, Saying with a loud voice, Fear God, and give glory to him; for the hour of his judgment is come: and worship him that made heaven, and earth, and the sea, and the fountains of waters. (Revelation 14:6–7)

If the gospel is preached, then salvation is available. If salvation is available, then the Holy Spirit must be available to consummate the union between Jesus and the repentant. "Nevertheless I tell you the truth; It is expedient for you that I go away: for if I go not away, the Comforter will not come unto you; but if I depart, I will send him unto you. And when he is come, he will reprove the world of sin, and of righteousness, and of judgment: Of sin, because they believe not on me; Of righteousness, because I go to my Father, and ye see me no more; Of judgment, because the prince of this world is judged" (John 16:7–11).

The Holy Spirit has also been given to the believer as a personal guarantee that the believer is saved. "In whom ye also trusted, after that ye heard the word of truth, the gospel of your salvation: in whom also after that ye believed, ye were sealed with that holy Spirit of promise, Which is the earnest of our inheritance until the redemption of the purchased possession, unto the praise of his glory" (Ephesians 1:13–14).

2

The Holy Spirit has to be in the earth for the repentant to be saved. He's the guarantee of our inheritance and the one who will convict the world of sin, of righteousness, and of judgment. Without the working of the Spirit, there is no salvation.

Furthermore, if only the Holy Spirit is taken out of the earth, then He has forsaken the church. And that is impossible. "If ye love me, keep my commandments. And I will pray the Father, and he shall give you another Comforter, that he may abide with you for ever; Even the Spirit of truth; whom the world cannot receive, because it seeth him not, neither knoweth him: but ye know him; for he dwelleth with you, and shall be in you. I will not leave you comfortless: I will come to you" (John 14:15–18).

I cannot agree with this doctrine because the scriptures refute it.

The Church Is Restraining Lawlessness until the Rapture

Next, I've heard that it is the church that is restraining the lawlessness in the world and that when the rapture occurs, the restraint will be released, and then the Antichrist will be revealed. I have this question: How can the rapture release the restraint when it doesn't occur until after the lawless one is revealed? In other words, the lawless one is revealed, and then the rapture occurs (the rapture being the return of Jesus for His people).

Let me show you why I ask.

Remember in 2 Thessalonians 2:7–8 (NKJV), "He who now restrains will do so until He is taken out of the way. And then the lawless one will be revealed." Now look at the beginning of 2 Thessalonians 2, which says,

> Now we beseech you, brethren, *by the coming of*
> *our Lord Jesus Christ, and by our gathering together*
> *unto him,* That ye be not soon shaken in mind, or
> be troubled, neither by spirit, nor by word, nor by
> letter as from us, as that the day of Christ is at hand.

> Let no man deceive you by any means: for *that day*
> *shall not come, except* there come a falling away first,
> and *that man of sin be revealed*, the son of perdition.
> (2 Thessalonians 2:1–3; emphasis mine)

"That day shall not come except ... that man of sin be revealed!" Here the Holy Spirit declares that the coming of the Lord and our gathering together to Him will not happen until *after* the lawless one is revealed. In other words, the rapture takes place after the Antichrist is revealed. Therefore, the rapture can't be the mechanism that allows the Antichrist to be revealed.

The rapture isn't something that's taken out of the way. The rapture is an event that takes place.

What is the divine order of the end times? Who or what is restraining the lawless one? What do other scriptures bear witness to? Can this doctrine be found in Jesus's teachings and in the teachings of the apostles? Does the book of Revelation read this way? Is eschatology easier to understand than our current doctrines? These questions are the basis of this study.

The Troubled Church

"Now, brethren, concerning the coming of our Lord Jesus Christ and our gathering together to Him, we ask you, not to be soon shaken in mind or troubled, either by spirit or by word or by letter, as if from us, as though the day of Christ had come" (2 Thessalonians 2:1–2 NKJV).

The apostle Paul, in a heartfelt concern for the church at Thessalonica, wrote them a letter with the intent of comforting their souls and correcting the doctrine that had brought them the discomfort.

What had shaken this church? Why were the Thessalonians troubled?

They were afraid that *the day of Christ had come.* They believed that Jesus had come and left them here. That indeed would be a reason to be shaken in mind and troubled. But by inspiration of the Holy Spirit, Paul set everything straight. He gave them signposts to look for. Furthermore, he declared that to believe anything other than what he was about to write would mean that they had been deceived. "Let no man deceive you by any means" (2 Thessalonians 2:3).

God doesn't want His people to be deceived. Therefore, He has given us clear warning and markers to follow.

What to Look For

As we continue in 2 Thessalonians, we see in verse 3 that there are two prominent signs that the Holy Spirit instructs us to look for prior to the coming of the Lord. "Let no man deceive you by any means: for that day shall not come, except there come a falling away first, and that man of sin be revealed" (2 Thessalonians 2:3).

The two signs are (1) the falling away first and (2) the man of sin revealed. To believe that Jesus will come prior to these events is to be deceived.

The Falling Away

Falling away in the Greek is *apostasia*, meaning the rebellion or departure. It is where we get our word *apostasy*, which means abandonment of one's religious faith, political party, or cause.

Keep in mind that a person cannot depart from somewhere if he or she wasn't there in the first place. I cannot depart from a building if I was never in the building. Nor can there be a rebellion against someone who doesn't have jurisdiction over those rebelling. I can't rebel against your boss because he or she has no authority over me. But I can rebel against my boss because he has a certain amount of authority over me at work.

In other words, God is warning us that there will be those who forsake the holy covenant (Christians) and become apostates. There will be those who fall away from the faith and give heed to seducing spirits and doctrines of demons. "Now the Spirit speaketh expressly, that in the latter times some shall depart from the faith, giving heed to seducing spirits, and doctrines of devils" (1 Timothy 4:1).

I can't emphasize enough that these are Christian people who get wrapped up in false beliefs that turn them away from the truth. These false beliefs may appear religious and humane, but they are actually lies designed to deceive the listener. They may believe they're doing the right thing, but they're persecuting other Christians and making a path for the destroyer. Counterfeiters don't replicate three-dollar bills. Why? There are no three-dollar bills. They only counterfeit bills that are in use. Likewise, liars tell enough truth to make their deception believable to the simple-minded—or in this case, to those with unrenewed minds. "Be not conformed to this world: but be ye transformed by the renewing of your mind, that ye may prove what is that good, and acceptable, and perfect, will of God" (Romans 12:2). A mind in alignment with the Word of God is a mind that is renewed and can prove what God's will is. If you don't know what the truth is, you can't tell what a counterfeit is.

When tempted by the devil, Jesus was quoted scripture meant to deceive Him: "Then the devil taketh him up into the holy city, and setteth him on a pinnacle of the temple, And saith unto him, If thou be the Son of God, cast thyself down: for it is written, He shall give his angels charge concerning thee: and in their hands they shall bear thee up, lest at any time thou dash thy foot against a stone. Jesus said unto him, It is written again, Thou shalt not tempt the Lord thy God" (Matthew 4:5–7).

It is true that the scripture says this. The devil is quoting from the Psalm 91. So where's the deception? Jesus couldn't do it by faith. God hadn't commanded Jesus to jump off a cliff. Nor did Jesus accidentally slip. If Jesus were to have jumped, it would have been His decision alone. He would have jumped to His death because He chose to do it. Later on we see Jesus walking on the water. What's the difference? Jumping off the cliff would have been a personal

6

decision that God wasn't obligated to support. Walking on the water was a supernatural manifestation of the Holy Spirit because of Jesus's obedience. Jesus knew God's will was for Him to walk on the water.

Confidence men (con men), counterfeiters, and other deceivers will use lures for you to bite into so they can capture you in their schemes. There are many attractive lures that we all have to be vigilant about. And the only way to recognize the real is to spend time with God through His word, prayer, and Spirit. Don't be in a rush to believe or follow anyone. God will bear witness to His truth many times as you stay in fellowship with Him.

The Man of Sin Revealed

How do we recognize the man of sin?

Second Thessalonians 2:4, 9–10 says, "Who opposeth and exalteth himself above all that is called God, or that is worshipped; so that he as God sitteth in the temple of God, shewing himself that he is God. Even him, whose coming is after the working of Satan with all power and signs and lying wonders, And with all deceivableness of unrighteousness in them that perish; because they received not the love of the truth, that they might be saved."

What a list!

1. He opposes and exalts himself above all that is called God or that is worshipped.
2. He sits as God in the temple of God, showing himself that he is God.
3. He comes according to the working of Satan with all power, signs, lying wonders, and unrighteous deception.

He believes that he is God and expects everyone else to worship him. Satan throws his power behind this man and causes miracles to occur. The objective is to deceive the world into believing that he's their only help.

If you're already looking for a human being to make your life easier, you're on the wrong track. What a man or government gives you, he'll use to put you in bondage. Or rather Satan will by him. Romans 6:16 says, "Know ye not, that to whom ye yield yourselves servants to obey, his servants ye are to whom ye obey; whether of sin unto death, or of obedience unto righteousness?" To be clear, I'm talking about faith, attitude, and lifestyle. Obtaining help isn't wrong. We all need help at times. Relying on and putting our trust in humans for sustenance and happiness creates a lifestyle of self-induced slavery and an entitlement attitude, and living off other people's work is not from God. We are to be people of faith in God supplying our needs (Philippians 4:19). We are to be people of prayer, expecting God to guide those in authority on our behalf (1 Timothy 2:1–2). Our attitude should be that we are the blessed and God will bless others through us (Genesis 12:2–3; Romans 4:13–16). Use caution and prayer when trusting in human ways of deliverance. Always support rulers with prayer. Who would God vote for? Who honors Him or His ways? God honors His word and will also bless those who honor it. The chief deception of the Antichrist is his lie that he can create a prosperous, united world.

The Spirit of God has warned us that these two events must take place before the coming of the Lord. As we go further into the study of eschatology, we'll see how Jesus, the prophets, and the apostles confirm, reiterate, and expand these events.

The Coming of the Lord and Our Gathering Together

Second Thessalonians 2:1 says, "Now we beseech you, brethren, by the coming of our Lord Jesus Christ, and by our gathering together unto him."

Let's discuss what "the coming of our Lord Jesus Christ and by our gathering together unto him" means. Keep in mind that the New Testament was in the process of being written. Paul wanted to put the Thessalonians on the right track so that they wouldn't be deceived. Because the New Testament was in the process of being written, the Thessalonians had to rely on the prophecies of the Old Testament and the teaching of the apostle. They couldn't go to the book of Revelation. It wouldn't be written for another thirty-nine years. It's amazing to me how some want to start off with the book of Revelation, and they put little emphasis on what the apostles wrote. There's little wonder why so much confusion exists on this subject. Here's the most important event since the resurrection, and no one wants to discuss it or even has much understanding about it.

If you had to travel due south by a compass to reach your destination and you started on a bearing of 181 degrees instead of 180, it wouldn't make much difference at first. But the further you traveled, the further off course you'd become until there was no way of reaching your destination. So it is with doctrine. If our base is skewed, then the further we get away from the base, then the more skewed the doctrine gets. Finding out what the apostles had written prior to John's Revelation will help us keep our bearings as we traverse the book of Revelation. What the apostles and prophets wrote will agree with the book of Revelation.

It is important to note what Paul had previously written to the Thessalonians, because his intentions were to put the Thessalonians back on the right track. This is evidenced in verse 5. Second Thessalonians 2:5 says, "Remember ye not, that, when I was yet with you, I told you these things?"

The Thessalonians had been taught this already but had forgotten. Let's take a look at what Paul previously taught them. First Thessalonians 4:13–18 says,

> But I would not have you to be ignorant, brethren, concerning them which are asleep, that ye sorrow not, even as others which have no hope. For if we believe that Jesus died and rose again, even so them also which sleep in Jesus will God bring with him. For this we say unto you by the word of the

Lord, that we which are alive and remain unto the coming of the Lord shall not prevent them which are asleep. For the Lord himself shall descend from heaven with a shout, with the voice of the archangel, and with the trump of God: and the dead in Christ shall rise first: Then we which are alive and remain shall be caught up together with them in the clouds, to meet the Lord in the air: and so shall we ever be with the Lord. Wherefore comfort one another with these words.

As we read verses 15 through 17, we can see what Paul means by the "coming of the Lord." In other words, what happens when the Lord returns? First Thessalonians 4:15–17 says,

For this we say unto you by the word of the Lord, that we which are alive and remain unto *the coming of the Lord* ... For the Lord himself shall descend from heaven with a shout, with the voice of the archangel, and with the trump of God: and the dead in Christ shall rise first: Then we which are alive and remain shall be caught up together with them in the clouds, to meet the Lord in the air: and so shall we ever be with the Lord. (emphasis mine)

What happens when Jesus comes again? The dead in Christ will rise first, and then the rest will be caught up together with them.

Notice in verse 15 the phrase "the coming of the Lord." Also in verse 17, the phrases "caught up" and "so shall we ever be with the Lord." It is obvious that these phrases are identifying the same event. In other words, when the Lord comes, we will be caught up to Him and shall always be with the Lord from that point on.

Look in chapter 5, and keep in mind that these chapters (4 and 5) were separated by scholars; however, in the original documents, they flowed together. First Thessalonians 5:1–2 says, "But of the times and the seasons, brethren, ye have no need that I write unto you. For yourselves know perfectly that the day of the Lord so cometh as a thief in the night."

In verse 2, Paul uses the term "the day of the Lord." He's using the "coming of the Lord," "caught up," and "the day of the Lord" interchangeably. Therefore, in 1 Thessalonians 4–5, Paul uses the "coming of the Lord" and the "day of the Lord" synonymously.

Now we look again in 2 Thessalonians 2. We read "the coming of our Lord Jesus Christ," "our gathering together to Him," "the day of Christ," and "that Day." Here, these must reference one eventful *day*, a time when Jesus comes and we're raised to meet Him. This is one event and not one *coming* to get the faithful and another *coming* to get those who come out of the great tribulation. It wouldn't do for Paul to use the same terminology to mean different events. The Thessalonians were already confused and didn't remember what was previously taught. To throw something in other than what was already taught would cause insurmountable confusion.

Here's a quick synopsis: The great tribulation begins, and at the end of the tribulation, Jesus returns and *raptures* His own. The wrath of God is poured out. The battle of Armageddon takes place. Then Jesus sets up His government on the planet, and the millennial reign begins. This will become clearer as we proceed.

God wants us in the light and not in the dark (1 Thessalonians 5:1–10). When the Holy Spirit inspired Paul to write to the Thessalonians, He kept it simple. "The coming of the Lord," "the coming of our Lord Jesus Christ," "our gathering together to Him," and "the day of Christ" are one event in these letters.

What Is Restraining?

Second Thessalonians 2:6–8 says, "And now ye know what withholdeth that he might be revealed in his time. For the mystery of iniquity doth already work: only he who now letteth will let, until he be taken out of the way. And then shall that Wicked be revealed, whom the Lord shall consume with the spirit of his mouth, and shall destroy with the brightness of his coming."

Reread verses 7 and 8, and take note that the lawless one cannot be revealed *until* "he who now restrains is taken out of the way" "He who now restrains will do so until He is taken out of the way. And then the lawless on will be revealed" (NKJV).

Now I've always heard it preached that it is the church being taken out of the way through the rapture or that the Holy Spirit is taken out of the earth. I disagree with both.

What about the Lord's returning (rapture) being the event that takes off the restraint? Remember verse 3? The Lord will not come until there comes (1) a falling away and (2) the lawless one is revealed (2 Thessalonians 2:1–3).

Since the Lord will not come until after the lawless one is revealed, then the Lord's return cannot be the event that takes off the restraint and reveals the lawless one!

It's important that you see that. The lawless one has to be revealed before the Lord comes; therefore, the church has to be here when the lawless one is revealed. This sets the direction to take for accurate doctrine. This keeps confusion in check.

So many Christians are looking to be rescued (by the rapture) from the great tribulation that they're unprepared for what will come. In fact, I've been hard-pressed to find anyone who wants to discuss the end times or anyone who can scripturally defend their position. We need to stop being ignorant. We need to be sure that we're not deceived. We need to get a warrior mentality and be prepared for whatever may come.

Let me ask you this: Who wants no restraints? God? Does God want there to be lawlessness? Does God want sin to abound? Does God want millions of people to go into eternity without Jesus? No, God does not. God instructs us to pray for all men and for those in authority so that the gospel can be preached and people will be saved (1 Timothy 2:1–2).

So who wants the restraints taken off? Who wants to be lawless? Who doesn't want God in their thinking or wants to be restrained by godliness? It certainly isn't God. It's the ungodly, the Antichrist, the *son of perdition*, the *lawless one*, and those who want to follow him. *The mystery of iniquity (lawlessness) is already at work.* In other words, there's a push to get God out of the way so that they can do what they want to do (Romans 1:18, 28–32).

What is restraining lawlessness? The church! The church is the salt of the earth (Matthew 5:13). The church is the light of the world (Matthew 5:14). The church is the ambassador to the unsaved (2 Corinthians 5:20). If the church is taken out of the way, then lawlessness is the only recourse.

How then is the church taken out of the way? Consider who wants the church out of their way. It is those who love sin. It is the Antichrist and those who are antichrist (those who are against Christ).

How then is the church taken out of the way? Concerning the lawless one that will arise and be moved against God's people, the scriptures have this to say: "Then shall he return into his land with great riches; and his heart shall be against the holy covenant; and he shall do exploits, and return to his own land ... And such as do wickedly against the covenant shall he corrupt by flatteries: but the people that do know their God shall be strong, and do exploits" (Daniel 11:28, 32).

The Antichrist is looking for those who will act wickedly against God's people. Revelation 13:7 says, "And it was given unto him to make war with the saints, and to overcome them: and power was given him over all kindreds, and tongues, and nations."

As a note, it isn't God who's granting this man any authority or power. It is the kingdoms of the world, and they have been deceived by Satan. I'll say this about apostasy at this time. Because of tremendous persecution, there will be those who leave their first love and persecute and betray other believers.

Daniel 11:30 says, "For the ships of Chittim shall come against him: therefore he shall be grieved, and return, and have indignation against the holy covenant: so shall he do; he shall even return, and have intelligence with them that forsake the holy covenant." And 2 Thessalonians 2:3 says, "Let no man deceive you by any means: for that day shall not come, except there come a falling away first, and that man of sin be revealed, the son of perdition."

Jesus spoke much about this in Matthew's gospel, and there's more to be said about this; however, we'll save that for other chapters. I want to give you a condensed outline of Revelation 12:7–13:18 in order to make clear the events that will take shape so that the lawless one can be revealed.

Revelation 12:7–13:18 (Outline)

1. Satan is driven from his heavenly position above the earth by the authority of the saints and the warring angels. This is how he knows that his time is short and the reason he's willing to share his power with a man (the Antichrist) (12:7–12).
2. He brings stiff persecution against the church (12:13–17).
3. Satan gives his authority to the Antichrist (13:4).
4. The Antichrist (Beast) declares war on the saints (13:7).
5. The false prophet arises, and then the abomination of desolation occurs. This is when the lawless one is revealed (13:14–15).
6. The institution of the mark of the Beast is the final blow to breaking all restraints (13:16–18; Daniel 12:7).

Let me summarize this. When Paul wrote to the Thessalonians, he was reiterating what he had already taught them. They were confused and had fallen prey to false doctrine. Paul gave them two signposts to be aware of, namely (1) apostasy and (2) the revealing of the Antichrist at the time of the abomination of desolation. He also revealed that the *rapture* of the church could not happen until the

Antichrist was revealed. It is also important to note that Paul didn't mix phrases, names, and events with other meanings. In other words, when he mentioned the coming of the Lord as he explained it in his first letter to the Thessalonians, he kept the meaning in his second letter to them.

CHAPTER 2

 ⊷⇒◯ ⊜⇒⊶

Matthew 24 and 25

Matthew 24

The Beginning: Matthew 24:4–8

Matthew 24:4–8 says, "And Jesus answered and said unto them, Take heed that no man deceive you. For many shall come in my name, saying, I am Christ; and shall deceive many. And ye shall hear of wars and rumours of wars: see that ye be not troubled: for all these things must come to pass, but the end is not yet. For nation shall rise against nation, and kingdom against kingdom: and there shall be famines, and pestilences, and earthquakes, in divers places. All these are *the beginning* of sorrows" (emphasis mine).

"Take heed that no one deceives you!" Jesus put the responsibility in our hands. Are we being deceived? In what can we be deceived? Who or what are we following and receiving as the truth? It is our responsibility to know the truth: Ephesians 5:17 says, "Wherefore be ye not unwise, but understanding what the will of the Lord is." In case you haven't figured it out, this is why we have the Bible, the Holy Spirit, and anointed ministers of God. Put the Word first, and judge your beliefs by it.

Jesus said, "All these are the beginning of sorrows." What things? Let's take a brief look at what He said.

First, He said, "For many shall come in my name, saying, I am Christ; and shall deceive many." I take this statement to mean two things. There will be those who claim to be Jesus, and second, there will be those who claim to have the answers to the world's problems.

I think that many of us are unaware of how prevalent this is. There are many false Christs and false witnesses for Christ that we come in contact with in our daily lives. They may come in the guise of politicians, eco groups, influential musicians and entertainers, religious leaders, or some other symbol of a savior. They bring with them doctrines claiming that they know the way to peace, salvation of the earth, and world prosperity. They deny there is a God. Or if they *believe* in God, they deny any sort of judgment. There are religious leaders that believe in Jesus but preach that Jesus was a homosexual and that such a lifestyle is scriptural. The entertainment business promotes every sort of special interest and thinks nothing of defaming Jesus and Christians. Such people partake of and enjoy the world's system (Babylon) and deny the Word of God.

Many have followed their ways blindly. One only has to look at the way many Christians vote to see that such deception has crept into the people of God. Instead of basing decisions on God's word, they have based it on what they believe will be in their best economic interest, race, gender, or favorite entertainer's view. Amazing!

Jesus also said, "And ye shall hear of wars and rumours of wars." There are wars going on all over the world. They are in the news daily. Because of the effect of the vast, worldwide communications, great stress is caused by hearing these things. Such stress adds to the seeking of a *savior.*

Third, He said, "For nation shall rise against nation, and kingdom against kingdom." This may refer to both outward strife and inward strife. An example of outward strife would be Israel against Iran. An inward strife example would be domestic terrorists, such as an ecology-based group, causing destruction within the United States.

So too, Jesus once stated, "There shall be famines, and pestilences, and earthquakes, in divers places." These things have always existed. What makes this pertinent is this is the first time in history that we can know of the things *in various places.* Not just the locals know about what's happening.

Jesus said, "All these are the beginning of sorrows." The word *sorrow* means (*Strong's Exhaustive Concordance*) "a pang or throe, especially of childbirth: pain, sorrow, travail." *Webster's Dictionary* defines sorrow as "(1) mental suffering caused by loss, disappointment, etc.; sadness, grief, or regret; to worry or be ill. (a) Very hard work; toil. (b) Labor pains; pains of childbirth."

The knowledge of all these things happening is causing stress and mental suffering. It's causing stress without a way for the world to release it. Because these *sorrows* are known daily via worldwide media outlets, the stress is intensified. More to the point, these things indicate that something new is to be born. They're birth pangs that are happening at the end of this age and ushering in a new millennial age with Jesus as Lord of the earth.

Keep in mind that the "end is not yet" (verse 6). In fact, the first thing that Jesus said was, "Take heed that no one deceives you" (verse 4). Why would He say that? I used to wonder how anyone could be deceived with such precise information. It has since become clear. People want to see what they want and will ignore the truth. Peter wrote, "For they willfully overlook and forget" (2 Peter 3:5 AMP[1]). They willfully overlook and forget God and anything in His word that they disagree with. Jesus is speaking to His disciples as He gave us this warning.

---

[1] Scripture quotations taken from the Amplified Bible, Copyright 1954, 1958, 1962, 1964, 1965, 1987 by the Lockman Foundation. Used by permission (www.Lockman.org).

Matthew 24:3 says, "And as he sat upon the Mount of Olives, the disciples came unto him."

Jesus spoke to Peter, James, John, and the others and said, "Take heed that no one deceives you." There are those who argue that Jesus was speaking to the Jews (non-Christians). As a nation, the Jews have never accepted Jesus as Lord and Messiah. *They're already deceived.* Therefore, Jesus can't be speaking to the Jews. Furthermore, the scripture states that Jesus was speaking to His disciples. Are you His disciple? Is the body of Christ divided? Didn't Jesus break "down the middle wall of partition" between the believing Jews and believing Gentiles, making us one body in him (Ephesians 2:11–22)?

Consider verse 9. Speaking to His disciples, Jesus said that they would be hated by all because they believed in Him. This clarifies to whom Jesus was addressing, specifically those who believe in Him.

Jesus is indeed warning believers not to be deceived! Jesus made it our responsibility not to be deceived, and He gave us His word and His Spirit to help us keep on the correct path. Jesus asked a very dramatic question, "Nevertheless when the Son of man cometh, shall he find faith on the earth?" (Luke 18:8).

That is a question that the individual must ask him or herself. Faith comes by hearing the word of God (Romans 10:17). God's word reveals His will for us. A deceived person is one who believes something other than God's word. In the different aspects of our lives (political, social, financial, family, etc.), it's God's word that keeps us from deception. The time of the end is a time when deception will abound. Why? It's because people will refuse to guide their affairs by the Bible.

Persecution: Matthew 24:9–14

Matthew 24:9 says, "Then shall they deliver you up to be afflicted, and shall kill you: and ye shall be hated of all nations for my name's sake." I always notice the word *then*. Obviously, during the chaotic time that He had just spoken of, they will persecute the believers. In fact, Jesus reveals that we will be hated *by all nations*. This is a worldwide situation. The persecution will be so great that Jesus forewarns of an apostasy.

Matthew 24:10–13 says, "And then shall many be offended, and shall betray one another, and shall hate one another. And many false prophets shall rise, and shall deceive many. And because iniquity shall abound, the love of many shall wax cold. But he that shall endure unto the end, the same shall be saved."

What causes many to be offended? And who are they offended with? Many will be offended because of the persecution that they must confront for confessing the name of Jesus. "And ye shall be hated of all nations for my name's sake" (Matthew 24:9). They will hate us because we preach salvation through Jesus alone. In Mark 4:17, Jesus said that Satan attacks with tribulation and persecution to stop the word of God. Remember, Jesus asked if He would find faith in the earth when He came. We must ask ourselves, "Are we willing to stand on God's word during tribulation and persecution?"

So if it's tribulation and persecution that offend *many* (I emphasize *many* because you may not be one of them), who are they offended with? Those who won't compromise their faith— that's who. The offended becomes the offender toward those who won't believe as they do.

Matthew 24:10, 12 (NKJV) says, "And then many will be offended, will betray one another, and will hate one another … And because lawlessness will abound, the love of many will grow cold." Matthew 24:12 (William's translation) says, "Because of the increasing crime wave, most people's love will grow cold." Matthew 24:12 (Beck's translation) says, "Because there will be more and more wickedness, the love of most people will turn cold."

We see this happening now. Because of the increase in crime, bribery, persecution of righteousness, and evil deeds, people are becoming more frightened and panicked. The future has little hope. The desire for a savior is on the rise. The world is looking for someone who will bring peace and prosperity. Persecution toward those who stand in the way of the belief that humans can fix the world's problems has increased. There has been an increase of people who have become insensitive to God and are looking for a human to take control. Those who preach salvation in Jesus alone face more criticism.

There are Christians who have fallen prey to the ideals of humanism and the abilities of man to fix the world's problems without godliness. Such thoughts twist the thinking to the point that they take sides with the spirit of antichrist. Slow desensitizing can bring about apostasy.

This is the apostasy that Paul wrote to the Thessalonians about. Second Thessalonians 2:3 says, "Let no man deceive you by any means: for that day shall not come, except there come a falling away (*apostasy*) first, and that man of sin be revealed, the son of perdition" (emphasis mine).

Realize that the time that Jesus is warning about has never been before nor shall ever be again. There's nothing new under the sun, such as the time of Noah, but nothing as extreme as this era. Lawlessness will be rampant, and the love of many will grow cold. (Many will become desensitized.) The word *love* is the Greek word *agape*. This is the Greek word that the scriptures use to describe love as God shows toward us. This is the love we're commanded to live by. We could restate Matthew 24:10, 12 as such: "Because lawlessness will abound, the commandment to love one another will grow cold and they will betray one another, and will hate one another." The Scripture says that the love of God has been poured out in our hearts by the Holy Spirit, who was given to us. The Holy Spirit hasn't been given to those who have not accepted Jesus; therefore, the love of God has not been poured out in their hearts. This being the case, those who don't have the love of God in their hearts can't allow that love to get cold. They don't have God's love in the first place. Jesus is speaking to His disciples. That's not to say that those in the world won't become more hard-hearted. Of course they will. As times become more troubling, people become more and more concerned with self-preservation and more desensitized toward others, especially toward those who disagree with them (those they feel are a cause to the problems).

I want to interject this. There is a difference between a student and a disciple. Students study the word. They enjoy talking about how they overcame this or how they did that. They seem to be looking for recognition for accomplishments though they would never admit to it or may not even realize it. They haven't yet realized that what they boasted about overcoming may have been created by their own faults. Most of the time they say they believe God's word but fail to put it into practice in all the affairs of their lives. The disciple, on the other hand, studies so that he can do the words of the master. He is very much aware that it was his master that taught and guided him through the difficult areas of life—some of which were self-created. He's grateful to the master for the master's love, guidance, and power that hallmarks his life. Boasting of oneself isn't even considered. The scriptures are studied in order to do them.

It is interesting to note verse 11, which says, *"Then* many false prophets will rise up and deceive many" (Matthew 24:11 NKJV, emphasis mine)

The rise of many false prophets occurs as many fall away from the faith. The opportunity for satanic influence becomes greater because of the rejection of the truth and not making decisions based on God's word. Rejection of the truth leaves no alternative but deception. False prophets inspire rebellion against God's people and His ways. And just as the false prophets of old in Israel, they bring in *destructive heresies* as the apostle Peter warned. Second Peter 2:1–2 says, "But there were false prophets also among the people, even as there shall be false teachers among you, who privily shall bring in damnable heresies, even denying the Lord that bought them, and bring upon themselves swift destruction. And many shall follow their pernicious ways; by reason of whom the way of truth shall be evil spoken of."

The apostle Paul said it this way: "Now the Spirit speaketh expressly, that in the latter times some shall depart from the faith, giving heed to seducing spirits, and doctrines of devils; Speaking lies in hypocrisy; having their conscience seared with a hot iron" (1 Timothy 4:1–2).

What was it Jesus first said about the end times? "Take heed that no one deceives you" (Matthew 24:4). How is a person deceived? By not knowing or acting on the word of God. For example, in the United States, we vote to elect public officials. When we elect someone, we're not just electing a person but those who are backing that person. As voters, if we fail to act on God's word and vote in beliefs contrary to God's ideals, then we are deceiving ourselves. God isn't going to bless those who are causing harm to His disciples. Voting for people who persecute the body of Christ is taking sides with the devil. There's no blessing in that. How many in the body of Christ have voted in antichrist ideals? It is the word of God that is the foundation and guide for our lives, not political parties and special interest groups.

Matthew 24:13 says, "But he that shall endure unto the end, the same shall be saved." How do we endure to the end? By being disciples and not students. By making God's word final authority in our lives and testing everything by His word. By keeping the commandment of God (walking in love).

Matthew 24:14 says, "And this gospel of the kingdom shall be preached in all the world for a witness unto all nations; and then shall the end come." There's something that surprises me. Some speak as if this is that only thing left to happen before Jesus comes (verse 14), and they overlook everything else. This is not a promise of when Jesus can return, but it says that this must occur before He will return. Jesus is just telling us that everyone will have an opportunity to have eternal life. It's the witness of Jesus that sparks satanic persecution. Satan isn't going to stand by and let the gospel be preached without a fight. As we study, more will become clearer. But let it suffice for now that it is the army of God that does exploits in the name of Jesus and takes the gospel to the world. It is the army of God that corners Satan so that his last stand is to throw his power behind an Antichrist. It is the army of God that overcomes by the word of their testimony and the blood of the Lamb. The gospel is preached even during the great tribulation, and it's at the end of the tribulation, just before the wrath of God is poured out, that Jesus returns. The divine order of the end times includes the great tribulation and then the rapture. Next, the wrath of God is poured out, and finally, the millennial reign begins.

Great Tribulation: Matthew 24:15–28

Second, Thessalonians 2:3–4 says, "Let no man deceive you by any means: for that day shall not come, except there come a falling away first, and that man of sin be revealed, the son of perdition; Who opposeth and exalteth himself above all that is called God, or that is worshipped; so that he as God sitteth in the temple of God, shewing himself that he is God."

This is the other signpost that Paul warned the Thessalonians to look for before the coming of the Lord. Jesus warned of the same event in Matthew 24:15. Matthew 24:15–20 says,

> When ye therefore shall see the abomination of desolation, spoken of by Daniel the prophet, stand in the holy place, (whoso readeth, let him understand:) Then let them which be in Judaea flee into the mountains: Let him which is on the housetop not come down to take any thing out of his house: Neither let him which is in the field return back to take his clothes. And woe unto them that are with child, and to them that give suck in those days! But pray ye that your flight be not in the winter, neither on the sabbath day.

Jesus made explicit reference to "the abomination of desolation" as a signpost to indicate that His coming is near. What is the abomination of desolation? Paul wrote that it is when the "man of sin be revealed, the son of perdition; Who opposeth and exalteth himself above all that is called God, or that is worshipped; so that he as God sitteth in the temple of God, shewing himself that he is God."

Writing of the Antichrist, Daniel has to say this: "And arms shall stand on his part, and they shall pollute the sanctuary of strength, and shall take away the daily sacrifice, and they shall *place the abomination that maketh desolate*" (Daniel 11:31, emphasis mine).

Where will he place the abomination of desolation? Where the daily sacrifices take place, or as Paul wrote, "So that he as God sitteth in the temple of God, shewing himself that he is God." The abomination is placed in the temple of God. Revelation 13:15 describes, I believe, the abomination of desolation.

Revelation 13:15 says, "And he had power to give life unto the image of the beast, that the image of the beast should both speak, and cause that as many as would not worship the image of the beast should be killed." The Antichrist (Beast) defiles the sanctuary and calls himself God. Then he has an image made of himself and demands that his image be worshipped. Jesus said that we would see the abomination of desolation. This image is the abomination of desolation.

In Matthew 25:15, Jesus said, "When ye therefore shall see the abomination of desolation." The word *therefore* ties in the previously mentioned chaotic, stressful, and perilous period. It's during that period that the abomination of desolation will occur. It's during that time a worldly savior will be desired and Satan will have opportunity to bring about the *son of perdition*, the Antichrist.

In Matthew 24:16–20, we see the swiftness of destruction when the Beast moves to be the supreme ruler. Jesus uses the abomination of desolation as a giant sign. This event cannot be mistaken if anyone has any desire to know the truth. As Jesus declared before, "Take heed that no man deceives you," the opportunity for deception will be great. God's word is the measuring device to gauge events.

Let's continue. In verse 21, the key words are *for then*. The words *for then* indicate that what is to follow will happen after what just occurred. Now what just occurred? *The abomination of desolation.*

Matthew 24:21 says, "For then shall be great tribulation, such as was not since the beginning of the world to this time, no, nor ever shall be." Therefore, because of the abomination of desolation, there will be great tribulation. This is why it's called the abomination of desolation. It causes great desolation to happen on the earth. It's a time when everyone will have to make a final decision about Jesus. To worship the abomination of desolation is to eternally reject the Son of God. The great tribulation is a result of people reaping what they've been sowing. And though they don't like what they're sowing, their faith is in the Antichrist to deliver them instead of repentance toward God. When all have chosen, then God reveals His wrath on those who have refused to repent.

Matthew 24:22 says, "And except those days should be shortened, there should no flesh be saved: but for the elect's sake those days shall be shortened." Jesus isn't speaking of shorter twenty-four-hour days but the ending of the tribulation. In other words, God will not allow the tribulation to run its natural course, the end being the destruction of *all flesh*. Instead He'll bring it to a close for His people's sake.

Matthew 24:23–26 says, "Then if any man shall say unto you, Lo, here is Christ, or there; believe it not. For there shall arise false Christs, and false prophets, and shall shew great signs and wonders; insomuch that, if it were possible, they shall deceive the very elect. Behold, I have told you before. Wherefore if they shall say unto you, Behold, he is in the desert; go not forth: behold, he is in the secret chambers; believe it not."

There will be such deception that even the elect must be on guard against it. False christs and prophets will perform great signs and wonders as illustrated in 2 Thessalonians 2:9–12 and 2 Timothy 3:8.

So how will we know that it is Jesus?

Matthew 24:27 says, "For as the lightning cometh out of the east, and shineth even unto the west; so shall also the coming of the Son of man be." We will know Jesus is returning because He will be seen like the lightning is seen flashing from the east to the west.

Matthew 24:28 says, "For wheresoever the carcase is, there will the eagles be gathered together." What does this say to me? Jesus will come at a time when those on the earth are but a carcass slain by sin and rebellion. At that time He will gather His people together to partake of what's left over.

The Lord's Return: Matthew 24:29–31

Matthew 24:29 says, "Immediately after the tribulation of those days." This is an interesting bit of scripture. It says that *after* the tribulation, something will happen. Therefore, the things that He goes on to say have to happen at the end of the great tribulation (verse 21). What does Jesus have to say?

Matthew 24:29 goes on, "Immediately after the tribulation of those days shall the sun be darkened, and the moon shall not give her light, and the stars shall fall from heaven, and the powers of the heavens shall be shaken"

Jesus starts with this list:

1. The sun will be darkened.
2. The moon will not give its light.
3. The stars will fall from heaven.
4. And the powers of the heavens will be shaken.

He doesn't end there, but He does qualify His next statement. Matthew 24:30 says, "And then shall appear the sign of the Son of man in heaven: and then shall all the tribes of the earth mourn, and they shall see the Son of man coming in the clouds of heaven with power and great glory." The qualifier is *then*. After all that He listed, He says, "Then shall appear the sign of the Son of man in heaven ... and they shall see the Son of man coming in the clouds of heaven with power and great glory."

After Jesus is revealed, then He will gather His elect (or as we like to say, *rapture*). Matthew 24:31 says, "And He will send His angels with a great sound of a trumpet, and they will gather together His elect from the four winds, from one end of heaven to the other."

Can you see the relationships between 2 Thessalonians 2 and Matthew 24? What will take place is the revealing of the Antichrist, the tribulation, and then at the end of the tribulation, the rapture.

The Fig Tree: Matthew 24:32–36

I want you to keep in mind that the main thrust of Jesus's sermon was the warning, "Take heed that no man deceives you." This was the first thing that He said. The apostle Paul had the same warning for the Thessalonians when he said, "Let no man deceive you by any means" (2 Thessalonians 2:3). Going forward in this study, I think you'll see Jesus emphasize this even more through His parables.

Matthew 24:32–36 says,

> Now learn a parable of the fig tree; When his branch is yet tender, and putteth forth leaves, ye know that summer is nigh: So likewise ye, when ye shall see all these things, know that it is near, even at the doors. Verily I say unto you, This generation shall not pass, till all these things be fulfilled. Heaven and earth shall pass away, but my words shall not pass away. But of that day and hour knoweth no man, no, not the angels of heaven, but my Father only.

The key to this passage is actually found in verse 36. Only the father knows the exact day and hour that Jesus will return.

However, as we can know by the leaves on the trees that summer is near. In like manner, by the events Jesus has just explained, we can know the answers to the disciples' questions, "Tell us, when shall these things be? and what shall be the sign of thy coming, and of the end of the world?" (verse 3). We are supposed to be aware of the drawing nigh of our Lord's coming. We are not to be deceived!

I've always heard it preached that the fig tree mentioned here is symbolic of Israel. Not once during His sermon has Jesus mentioned Israel. He could have just instructed them to keep an eye on Israel and told them what to look for. But He didn't. He was talking to his *disciples* and gave instructions to those who declare *His name.*

Luke 21:29 says, "And he spake to them a parable; Behold the fig tree, and all the trees." In Luke's account of the same end-time sermon, Jesus said, "And all the trees." He instructed us to look at all the trees. The trees were nothing more than an example of foretelling events based on known phenomenon. What Jesus is telling us is to be aware of the instructions that He had just given and when we see these things happen (in particular the abomination of desolation), we should know that this generation will not pass away. In verse 35, He said, "My words shall not pass away." Why would He say that? Because He's declaring that He wants us to look at His word. His word is the guide line. *His word is the "fig tree" that we're supposed to observe.*

Days of Noah: Matthew 24:37–41

Matthew 24:37–39 says, "But as the days of Noe were, so shall also the coming of the Son of man be. For as in the days that were before the flood they were eating and drinking, marrying and giving in marriage, until the day that Noe entered into the ark, And knew not until the flood came, and took them all away; so shall also the coming of the Son of man be."

The scripture says that Noah was a preacher of righteousness (2 Peter 2:5). I'm sure that one of the things that Noah preached was that judgment was about to take place, that a flood was coming. As we know, no one was listening. Before Jesus returns, many of us will be preaching that His return is soon. Yet as in the days before the flood, people will still be going about their business. They will be taking care of their daily lives. They will be unconcerned about Jesus, judgment, and eternity. They will believe that Christians are delusional. They will be unprepared for the return of Christ just as those who were unprepared for the flood. Please don't think that there won't be a great end-time harvest because there shall be. I'm speaking more of a polarization between those who are for Jesus and those who are against Him.

Matthew 24:40–41 says, "Then shall two be in the field; the one shall be taken, and the other left. Two women shall be grinding at the mill; the one shall be taken, and the other left." People have a built-in way of becoming accustomed to their environment. We adjust to make things at the very least tolerable. Even during the great tribulation, people overlook what appears to us as obvious— that is, the scriptures declaring the signs of the time. But as it was in the days of Noah, when Jesus comes, those who aren't ready stay behind. Those who *endure to the end* shall be saved from the wrath of God and taken in the rapture.

The Master of the House: Matthew 24:42–51

Matthew 24:42 says, "Watch therefore: for ye know not what hour your Lord doth come." Again, this verifies Jesus's concern about the Christian community and stresses that He isn't preaching to Israel. Notice that He said, "Your Lord is coming." He's speaking to those who call Him Lord!

Watch means to keep awake, be vigilant, and to be alert. Saying *watch* is the same thing Jesus said earlier, "Do not be deceived." If we could cruise through life without a chance of deception, then Jesus wouldn't say we should *watch*. This again tells me that there is danger in not being alert. What are we believing, and why? Is it in the Bible and out of the mouth of two or three witnesses? How can we be prepared? Look at the book of Hebrews. Hebrews 12:1 says, "Let us lay aside every weight, and the sin which doth so easily beset us, and let us run with patience the race that is set before us."

What are things that weigh us down? They are things that aren't necessarily sin, but they distract us from God's plans, purposes, and pursuits. Such things may be entertainment (TV, music, games, etcetera), clubs, activities, work, friends, food/diet, or anything that weighs our hearts down and makes us spiritually dull. On the other hand, a sin is something that God has spoken explicitly against, such as lying, stealing, homosexuality and other sexual sins, and witchcraft and other occult practices. Galatians 5:19–21 is a good list of things practiced that are sinful.

Matthew 24:43–44 says, "But know this, that if the goodman of the house had known in what watch the thief would come, he would have watched, and would not have suffered his house to be broken up. Therefore be ye also ready: for in such an hour as ye think not the Son of man cometh."

Ask yourself if you are allowing your house to be broken into. Is there sin, strife, and various weighty ways keeping you from being alert? What are you allowing into your personal life and your family? Is your ark ready for your family to escape the *flood* to come? Have you taken your place in the body of Christ? I encourage you not to be discouraged. Wait on the Lord. Be at peace, and be open for direction for your life—what He wants you to do and when He wants you to do it. Don't make things up. Rest in the Lord, and know that God knows how to speak to you (John 10:3–5; Romans 8:16). God has a way of verifying what He tells you through the written word. Stay connected to God through His word and prayer.

Matthew 24:45–47 says, "Who then is a faithful and wise servant, whom his lord hath made ruler over his household, to give them meat in due season? Blessed is that servant, whom his lord when he cometh shall find so doing. Verily I say unto you, That he shall make him ruler over all his goods."

Who is a faithful and wise servant? Who will be blessed when Jesus comes? Certainly not those left behind, but those who are working on the things that God has given them to do. Each of us has something that God has assigned. It may be taking care of our family and supporting our local church, or it may be going into a specific ministry. God is looking for obedience. Each of us has a season for that call, a time to do one thing and prepare for the next thing. And that *thing* will always be *food in due season* for God's people. In other words, we're part of a larger whole, and we have something important to give to the whole. We may not think of it as important, but it is to God. And that is where our blessing is. "Blessed is that servant, whom his lord when he cometh shall find so doing. Verily I say unto you, That he shall make him ruler over all his goods."

Now that we've looked at a blessed servant, let's contrast him with an evil servant. Matthew 24:48–51 says, "But and if that evil servant shall say in his heart, My lord delayeth his coming; And shall begin to smite his fellowservants, and to eat and drink with the drunken; The lord of that servant shall come in a day when he looketh not for him, and in an hour that he is not aware of, And shall cut him asunder, and appoint him his portion with the hypocrites: there shall be weeping and gnashing of teeth."

Who is an evil servant? First, he's one who is unfaithful and unwise (contrast verse 45). He is one who persecutes other servants (believers). He chooses the world and not God by his deeds and actions. He may be a religious church member, but by persecuting God's people and siding with the sinner's ways, he has chosen Satan. The foolish man may not even realize the danger he's put himself in. He's fallen away (2 Timothy 3:1–5).

What is the outcome of the evil servant? Jesus will come on a day when he's not expecting. Jesus will cut him from the body of Christ. His portion in eternity is the same as the unbeliever—eternal fire and punishment.

I'd like to add this. There are three problems with the modern theology of a pretribulation rapture.

1. It doesn't line up with the Bible.
2. People aren't preparing their hearts and minds properly. Fear has many focused on escape rather than allowing the scriptures to become a source of comfort and strength.
3. The people I know—and probably throughout the body of Christ—aren't praying or reaching out to their saved loved ones who are "playing on the fence" (one foot in the world while professing Jesus). This is a dangerous place for your loved ones. Remember, Jesus admonished us not to be deceived and to stay alert for His coming. God intends to use the prayers of the saints to make corrections and prepare loved ones for His return. But if we're focused on the wrong things ourselves, we won't be open to God's will or see the necessity of praying for our loved ones. Tell me. Does it make sense for God to pull out of the earth during the most critical time in history all the mature and experienced soldiers and leave the babies and inexperienced to fend for themselves? Of course not! It appears to me that the doctrine of a pretribulation rapture is selfish and motivated by fear.

Jesus continues with this topic of end-time events in Matthew 25.

Matthew 25

The Ten Virgins: Matthew 25:1–13

Matthew 25:1 says, "Then shall the kingdom of heaven be likened unto ..." *Then* means "at that time." This passage says, "At that time the kingdom of heaven will be like ..." Think about that. Jesus isn't describing what the nations of the world will be like but what the kingdom of heaven will be like. *When asked about His coming, Jesus wasn't concerned about the kingdoms of the earth but about His people and their spiritual condition.* Remember, the first thing that Jesus said was, "Take heed that no one deceives you."

At that time the kingdom of heaven will be like what? Matthew 25:1–2 says, "Then shall the kingdom of heaven be likened unto ten virgins, which took their lamps, and went forth to meet the bridegroom. And five of them were wise, and five were foolish."

At that time the kingdom of heaven will be like ten virgins. Five of them were wise, and five were foolish. Notice that all of them had lamps and that all of them were waiting for the bridegroom. That tells us that they had this in common: They were all born again (lamps), and they were all waiting for the return of the Lord. But five were wise. Where have we heard that before? Who are considered wise?

Matthew 24:45 says, "Who then is a faithful and wise servant, whom his lord hath made ruler over his household, to give them meat in due season?" The wise are the ones who are faithful to obey God. They obey the commandment of love and are busy feeding God's sheep with their *gift.*

And who are the foolish virgins? They are the ones who are unfaithful to God. They don't obey the commandment of love and are too busy to give their share to the body of Christ. Matthew 24:48–49 says, "But and if that evil servant shall say in his heart, My lord delayeth his coming; And shall begin to smite his fellowservants, and to eat and drink with the drunken."

They will side with the world, even though it causes Christians harm. There are people who vote that way. Amazing! I'd like to say, "Please be cautious. Beware." "Be not deceived; God is not mocked: for whatsoever a man soweth, that shall he also reap. For he that soweth to his flesh shall of the flesh reap corruption; but he that soweth to the Spirit shall of the Spirit reap life everlasting" (Galatians 6:7–8).

Matthew 25:3 says, "They that were foolish took their lamps, and took no oil with them." The foolish virgins were playing Christian. They took there salvation and did nothing with it. They may even be religious (i.e., going to church, volunteering, and putting on a show). But they were living in unforgiveness, criticizing, backbiting, murmuring, and causing strife. The apostle Paul warns, "Having a form of godliness, but denying the power thereof: from such turn away" (2 Timothy 3:5).

To the contrary, consider the wise virgins. "But the wise took oil in their vessels with their lamps" (Matthew 25:4). The wise care about their responsibilities. They care about their relationship with the Lord and hence, the body of Christ. They spend time in the Word, praying and staying in the love of God.

In verse 5, we see that they all faced the same issues in life. "While the bridegroom tarried, they all slumbered and slept" (Matthew 25:5).

Remember in Matthew 24:29–31, it says a time will come when Christ's return becomes apparent. Then everyone wants to be ready. This also happened to the virgins.

Matthew 25:6–12 says,

> And at midnight there was a cry made, Behold, the bridegroom cometh; go ye out to meet him. Then all those virgins arose, and trimmed their lamps. And the foolish said unto the wise, Give us of your oil; for our lamps are gone out. But the wise answered, saying, Not so; lest there be not enough for us and you: but go ye rather to them that sell, and buy for yourselves. And while they went to buy, the bridegroom came; and they that were ready went in with him to the marriage: and the door was shut. Afterward came also the other virgins, saying, Lord, Lord, open to us. But he answered and said, Verily I say unto you, I know you not.

The foolish weren't ready for the Lord's return. They had no oil in their lamps. In other words, they were not spiritually ready. They had spent their time loving the things of the world and forsook their first love, Jesus. Because of this, they went to the righteous to ask them for help to make up for what they lacked. But the wise said no. There comes a time when one answers, "No, you caused this problem, and you have to take care of it." Essentially, that is what the wise said, "Go ye rather to them that sell, and buy for yourselves." They told them that they needed to go to the one who could justify them because they couldn't.

Those who were ready went with the Lord. It is important to note the conversation between the Lord and the foolish virgins. Matthew 25:11–12 says, "Afterward came also the other virgins, saying, Lord, Lord, open to us. But he answered and said, Verily I say unto you, I know you not."

If we deny Jesus, He will deny us. Second Timothy 2:11–13 says, "It is a faithful saying: For if we be dead with him, we shall also live with him: If we suffer, we shall also reign with him: if we deny him, he also will deny us: If we believe not, yet he abideth faithful: he cannot deny himself."

Matthew quotes Jesus affirming the same thing. Matthew 10:32–33 says, "Whosoever therefore shall confess me before men, him will I confess also before my Father which is in heaven. But whosoever shall deny me before men, him will I also deny before my Father which is in heaven."

Again Jesus confirms this truth. Matthew 7:15–23 says,

Beware of false prophets, which come to you in sheep's clothing, but inwardly they are ravening wolves. Ye shall know them by their fruits. Do men gather grapes of thorns, or figs of thistles? Even so every good tree bringeth forth good fruit; but a corrupt tree bringeth forth evil fruit. A good tree cannot bring forth evil fruit, neither can a corrupt tree bring forth good fruit. Every tree that bringeth not forth good fruit is hewn down, and cast into the fire. Wherefore by their fruits ye shall know them.

> Not every one that saith unto me, Lord, Lord, shall enter into the kingdom of heaven; but he that doeth the will of my Father which is in heaven. Many will say to me in that day, Lord, Lord, have we not prophesied in thy name? and in thy name have cast out devils? and in thy name done many wonderful works? And then will I profess unto them, I never knew you: depart from me, ye that work iniquity.

If we're not ready ourselves, how can we help (or even recognize) the condition of those we want with us in eternity with God? The pressure will be on to deny Christ before His return. I can't tell you how many people (especially ministers) turn off, walk away, and have belittled me just because I want to talk (in fellowship and not argue) about the return of my Lord. It amazes me that people have no revelation themselves, can't find or defend their point of view with the Bible, believe only what they want to happen, yet mock anyone who has legitimate questions that the word of God inspires. How can a person be prepared with that attitude?

The Talents: Matthew 25:13–30

Matthew 25:13, 14a says, "Watch therefore, for ye know neither the day nor the hour wherein the Son of man cometh. For the kingdom of heaven is as …" Again, Jesus is describing what the kingdom of heaven is like. He says that we need to watch for His coming, because we don't know when His coming will be. Keep in mind, though, that His discourse is to prepare us and to give us guidance to recognize the season of His coming. The key word in verse 13 is *watch*. Be alert, and keep your eyes open for the signs of the time.

So what is the kingdom of heaven like? Let's read on. Matthew 25:14 says, "For the kingdom of heaven is as a man travelling into a far country, who called his own servants, and delivered unto them his goods."

What's he saying here? Jesus sits at the right hand of God, and between the time of His ascension and His return, He's given each of us responsibilities. We are accountable to him for our attitudes and actions toward those responsibilities. Matthew validates this.

Matthew 15:15–25 says,

> And unto one he gave five talents, to another two, and to another one; to every man according to his several ability; and straightway took his journey. Then he that had received the five talents went and traded with the same, and made them other five talents. And likewise he that had received two, he also gained other two. But he that had received one went and digged in the earth, and hid his lord's money. After a long time the lord of those servants cometh, and reckoneth with them. And so he that had received five talents came and brought other five talents, saying, Lord, thou deliveredst unto me five talents: behold, I have gained beside them five talents more. His lord said unto him, Well done, thou good and faithful servant: thou hast been faithful over a few things, I will make thee ruler over many things: enter thou into the joy of thy lord. He also that had received two talents came and said, Lord, thou deliveredst unto me two talents: behold, I have gained two other talents beside them. His lord said unto him, Well done, good and faithful servant; thou hast been faithful over a few things, I will make thee ruler over many things: enter thou into the joy of thy lord. Then he which had received the one talent came and said, Lord, I knew thee that thou art an hard man, reaping where thou hast not sown, and gathering where thou hast not strawed: And I was afraid, and

went and hid thy talent in the earth: lo, there thou
hast that is thine.

Let's catch up.

Take note that he gave to each according to his own ability
(verse 15). In other words, he handed out responsibilities according
to what they were capable of achieving. We all mature differently,
in different ways, and at different times. God's not holding this
against us. Frankly, He doesn't care. He knows us intimately and
loves us dearly. He just wants us to act on what we know. The five-
and two-talent guys made use of what they had and increased. The
one-talent man buried what he had. Burying implies putting it out
of mind and not caring for the gift or the will of the Lord. He didn't
care about God's assignment but only what he wanted to do. He
buried the talent and went and did what he wanted. The others
weren't perfect and had to deal with the issues of life the same as
the one-talent guy. The difference is attitude.

The Lord returns to settle accounts. That's what judgment is
about. It is a time to settle accounts before going onto something
new. Businesses do inventory at the end of their fiscal year. Why?
They do so to settle last year's profits and loses, to close out the
year, and to know where they stand as they go into the new year.
The same applies with the coming of the Lord. He is going to settle
accounts, close out the age, and let His people know where they
stand as they go into a new millennium. This is the judgment of the
saints. This is not the judgment of the unrighteous. The scripture
says that judgment begins in the house of the Lord (1 Peter 4:17).

Second Corinthians 5:10 says, "For we must all appear before
the judgment seat of Christ; that every one may receive the things
done in his body, according to that he hath done, whether it be good
or bad." And First Corinthian 3:11–15 says,

> For other foundation can no man lay than that is
> laid, which is Jesus Christ. Now if any man build

> upon this foundation gold, silver, precious stones, wood, hay, stubble; Every man's work shall be made manifest: for the day shall declare it, because it shall be revealed by fire; and the fire shall try every man's work of what sort it is. If any man's work abide which he hath built thereupon, he shall receive a reward. If any man's work shall be burned, he shall suffer loss: but he himself shall be saved; yet so as by fire.

The gold, silver, and precious stones will come through the fire, and the wood, hay, and straw will be burned away. After the judgment we only take the good things in our lives into eternity. It's the start of a new beginning for us. Each having a clean life to enjoy in the presence of God—in perfect fellowship with God and each other. Praise the Lord!

So the faithful and wise servants gained a reward from the master. What happened to the unfaithful and foolish servant? Matthew 25:26–30 says,

> His lord answered and said unto him, Thou wicked and slothful servant, thou knewest that I reap where I sowed not, and gather where I have not strawed: Thou oughtest therefore to have put my money to the exchangers, and then at my coming I should have received mine own with usury. Take therefore the talent from him, and give it unto him which hath ten talents. For unto every one that hath shall be given, and he shall have abundance: but from him that hath not shall be taken away even that which he hath. And cast ye the unprofitable servant into outer darkness: there shall be weeping and gnashing of teeth.

Jesus called this servant "wicked and lazy." *Wicked* means that he's twisted in his ways—twisted out of line with God's word. It comes from the word *wick*, like a wick for a candle. This servant is also lazy. He will put no effort forth to accomplish any work. He likes entertainment and pleasure. He wouldn't apply himself to his responsibilities.

The five- and two-talent guys entered into the joy of the Lord. But the wicked and lazy servant was judged accordingly. He had an excuse (verses 24–25), but it wasn't valid. The Lord gave responsibility according to the servant's ability (verse 15). In fact, the servant condemned himself by his own testimony (verses 26–27). The master didn't even argue with the servant. The servant knew what was right and wrong.

What was the judgment on the wicked servant? It was outer darkness, weeping, and gnashing of teeth and the lake of fire. This servant had *fallen away*. Those who practice lawlessness are destroyed with the lawless, even though they call Jesus Lord. Remember, Jesus is referring to the days of the great tribulation and His return and what His servants do during this time. Also, keep in mind that in Matthew 25, Jesus is expounding on Matthew 24, especially verses 45–51.

The Separation of the Servants and the Settling of Accounts: Matthew 25:31–46

Matthew 25:31–32 says, "When the Son of man shall come in his glory, and all the holy angels with him, then shall he sit upon the throne of his glory: And before him shall be gathered all nations: and he shall separate them one from another, as a shepherd divideth his sheep from the goats."

What throne of glory is Jesus talking about? His throne during His millennial reign. Consider the context of His statement. He said,

1. When He **comes** in His glory.
2. All the holy angels with Him.
3. Then He will sit on the throne of His glory.

We know Jesus is seated at the right hand of God now, but He doesn't consider this the throne of His glory. He's speaking of the time of His return. The throne of His glory is here on the earth during the millennial reign. Verse 32 says that all nations will be gathered before Him. Why? Because this is when He takes possession of the kingdoms of the earth. Verse 31 is describing when He takes possession of His throne on the earth. In contrast, during the great white throne judgment, all the dead are gathered before Him, and death, Hades, and the dead are thrown into the lake of fire. The saints aren't even mentioned (Revelation 20:11–15).

The Separation of the Nations at the Rapture

Revelation 14:9–12 says,

> And the third angel followed them, saying with a loud voice, If any man worship the beast and his image, and receive his mark in his forehead, or in his hand, The same shall drink of the wine of the wrath of God, which is poured out without mixture into the cup of his indignation; and he shall be tormented with fire and brimstone in the presence of the holy angels, and in the presence of the Lamb: And the smoke of their torment ascendeth up for ever and ever: and they have no rest day nor night, who worship the beast and his image, and whosoever receiveth the mark of his name. Here is the patience of the saints: here are they that keep the commandments of God, and the faith of Jesus.

The rapture separates the sheep from the goats. The nations are separated. Everyone who receives the Beast as their savior is forever doomed, including the saints who forsake the *commandments of God and the faith of Jesus*. Order will return to the earth. The nations will have their place, and the boundaries will be fixed. But Jesus takes this a little further. He spends time to talk about the sheep and the goats.

The sheep are those who were wise and faithful servants, and the goats are the unwise and foolish servants. When I was young, we went to a petting zoo. At the zoo they had a pen that had goats and sheep along with other animals,. The sheep had recently been sheared. I couldn't tell the difference between the goats and the sheep, and the keeper pointed out the difference. This is the point that Jesus is getting across. There are those who look like sheep but are really wolves in sheep's clothing. At the time of His return, there will be no more mistaking those whose are His and who's playing Christian.

Matthew 25:33–40 says

> And he shall set the sheep on his right hand, but the goats on the left. Then shall the King say unto them on his right hand, Come, ye blessed of my Father, inherit the kingdom prepared for you from the foundation of the world: For I was an hungred, and ye gave me meat: I was thirsty, and ye gave me drink: I was a stranger, and ye took me in: Naked, and ye clothed me: I was sick, and ye visited me: I was in prison, and ye came unto me. Then shall the righteous answer him, saying, Lord, when saw we thee an hungred, and fed thee? or thirsty, and gave thee drink? When saw we thee a stranger, and took thee in? or naked, and clothed thee? Or when saw we thee sick, or in prison, and came unto thee? And the King shall answer and say unto them, Verily I say unto you, Inasmuch as ye have done it unto

one of the least of these my brethren, ye have done
it unto me.

In verse 40, Jesus reveals that He is concerned with how we
treat *His* family. This is the key to His dialogue. Jesus said, "Come
ye blessed of My Father" (verse 34). If you'll remember in Matthew
24:45–47, Jesus described who were the blessed. They are those who
are faithful and wise servants whom He finds doing His will when
He returns. Those who are doing the Lord's commandments will
inherit the kingdom and will be made a ruler with Jesus (Matthew
24:47; Revelation 2:26–27).

Matthew 25:41–46 says,

> Then shall he say also unto them on the left hand,
> Depart from me, ye cursed, into everlasting fire,
> prepared for the devil and his angels: For I was an
> hungred, and ye gave me no meat: I was thirsty,
> and ye gave me no drink: I was a stranger, and ye
> took me not in: naked, and ye clothed me not: sick,
> and in prison, and ye visited me not. Then shall
> they also answer him, saying, Lord, when saw we
> thee an hungred, or athirst, or a stranger, or naked,
> or sick, or in prison, and did not minister unto
> thee? Then shall he answer them, saying, Verily I
> say unto you, Inasmuch as ye did it not to one of
> the least of these, ye did it not to me. And these
> shall go away into everlasting punishment: but the
> righteous into life eternal.

Everlasting life and everlasting punishment is the concern
of Jesus's sermon. The righteous and loving servants inherit
everlasting life. The abusive, unloving, and unfaithful servants who
have fallen away along with those of the nations that have followed
the Antichrist are cast into everlasting punishment.

Can you see that the parable of the sheep and goats is set in the time of the end? It is of the works done toward believers during a time of crisis and tribulation. Of course, it has relevance to now. That's not the point. The point is that Jesus is answering the disciples' questions about the end and His coming.

Postmillennial Judgment

I think this parable can also be used to gain understanding of the postmillennial great white throne of judgment.

Revelation 20:1–3, 7–11, 15 says,

> And I saw an angel come down from heaven, having the key of the bottomless pit and a great chain in his hand. And he laid hold on the dragon, that old serpent, which is the Devil, and Satan, and bound him a thousand years, And cast him into the bottomless pit, and shut him up, and set a seal upon him, that he should deceive the nations no more, till the thousand years should be fulfilled: and after that he must be loosed a little season … And when the thousand years are expired, Satan shall be loosed out of his prison, And shall go out to deceive the nations which are in the four quarters of the earth, Gog and Magog, to gather them together to battle: the number of whom is as the sand of the sea. And they went up on the breadth of the earth, and compassed the camp of the saints about, and the beloved city: and fire came down from God out of heaven, and devoured them. And the devil that deceived them was cast into the lake of fire and brimstone, where the beast and the false prophet are, and shall be tormented day and night for ever and ever.

> And I saw a great white throne, and him that
> sat on it, from whose face the earth and the heaven
> fled away; and there was found no place for them ...
> And whosoever was not found written in the book
> of life was cast into the lake of fire.

We read that after the thousand-year reign of Christ, Satan must be released to deceive the nations again. We know that the saints who are resurrected will be free from sin and death and will not have to go through this judgment (they've already been judged). They won't have to face the *second death* either (Revelation 2:11).

So what happens when Jesus returns? Jesus raptures His own. While this is occurring, the wrath of God is poured out into the earth, and the Beast's armies gather to the place called Armageddon (Revelation 16:16), where they're obliterated from the earth. But we also know that there will be unbelievers who will not be killed upon the earth during the battle of Armageddon and the outpouring of the wrath of God and who have not worshipped the Beast. We know this because the populous that's left multiplies during the thousand-year reign of Christ "as the sand of the sea." Isaiah writes, "And I will punish the world for their evil, and the wicked for their iniquity; and I will cause the arrogancy of the proud to cease, and will lay low the haughtiness of the terrible. I will make a man more precious than fine gold; even a man than the golden wedge of Ophir. Therefore I will shake the heavens, and the earth shall remove out of her place, in the wrath of the Lord of hosts, and in the day of his fierce anger" (Isaiah 13:11–13).

Those who are left are very few. And Jesus and His people will rule over them. Revelation 2:26–27 says, "And he that overcometh, and keepeth my works unto the end, to him will I give power over the nations: And he shall rule them with a rod of iron; as the vessels of a potter shall they be broken to shivers: even as I received of my Father."

By the end of the millennial reign, they will be as the *sand of the sea.* This is when Satan is let loose to "deceive the nations which are in the four corners of the earth, Gog and Magog, to gather them to battle, whose number is as the sand of the sea."

God is no respecter of persons. He shows no partiality (Acts 10:34). Those growing up in the millennial reign are going to have to choose Jesus as the Son of God and accept Him as Lord and Savior under the same conditions that Adam and the rest of us have had to do. Will they continue in the truth or succumb to deception? Once they have all chosen, the Lord will separate the *goats* from the *sheep.* "He who overcomes, and keeps My works until the end" will be saved. Those who don't will be "cast into the lake of fire" (Revelation 20:15). This is the great white throne judgment. This is the end of the age of deception, the curse, and sin. The books are closed.

It's after the great white throne of judgment that a new heaven and new earth are created (and we get to see it happen). Everyone has chosen. The sheep are with the Great Shepherd. The rebellious are in the kingdom of darkness, which is cast into the lake of fire.

When we studied "The Coming of the Lord and What to Look For," we learned that what the apostles wrote, what Jesus said, and what the prophets wrote must all agree. There is agreement with Jesus's dialogue and Paul's exhortation in 2 Thessalonians 2. What Paul wrote was condensed and designed to bring out two main events that herald the Lord's return, namely an apostasy and the man of perdition revealed (abomination of desolation). Jesus expounded in Matthew 24 and 25 and gave us pretribulation, tribulation, and posttribulation events in the gospels.

CHAPTER 3

As the Days of Noah Were

Matthew 24:36–42

Matthew 24:36–42 says,

> But of that day and hour knoweth no man, no,
> not the angels of heaven, but my Father only. But
> as the days of Noe were, so shall also the coming
> of the Son of man be. For as in the days that were
> before the flood they were eating and drinking,
> marrying and giving in marriage, until the day
> that Noe entered into the ark, And knew not until
> the flood came, and took them all away; so shall
> also the coming of the Son of man be. Then shall
> two be in the field; the one shall be taken, and the
> other left. Two women shall be grinding at the
> mill; the one shall be taken, and the other left.
> Watch therefore: for ye know not what hour your
> Lord doth come.

As mentioned earlier, this scripture is primarily concerned with
the apathy people will have concerning the coming of Jesus. People
will be concerned about their immediate state of affairs and the

cares of the world. But what were the days of Noah like. I believe that having an idea of Noah's situation will give us insight into the times we face—now and before Jesus' return.

I'm including a portion of a chapter from another book of mine to give you an idea of Noah's situation. I will only cover the first topic of the chapter.

Noah

Hebrews 11:7 says, "By faith Noah, being warned of God of things not seen as yet, moved with fear, prepared an ark to the saving of his house; by the which he condemned the world, and became heir of the righteousness which is by faith."

Noah was moved to action. He did something that corresponded with what he believed. God had warned Noah of impending judgment—something that Noah couldn't see or prove would come to pass. It was the word of God that he received in his heart that gave him hope—hope of rain, hope of judgment, hope of salvation, and hope of blessing.

We are creatures of faith. Everyone has faith, even unbelievers. One cannot *not* believe something. That something may be a lie, a deception, or that thing can be the word of God. Take Darwinism for instance. Those people think that they are standing on science, but they're actually full of faith. If you were to ask where the missing links are—let's say leading into the Cambrian Age—you will most likely hear someone say, "It's just a matter of time before it's discovered." That statement (or something similar) is where science ended and faith began. This person *believes* that he or she will find the links. There is no evidence to validate the statement. It's in the faith arena. An unbeliever isn't one without faith but one without faith in God's word.

Noah was moved by his faith. He prepared an ark without any scientific evidence. His faith was based solely on what God had said. God's word was the evidence of things hoped for. No one else may have believed the evidence, but Noah did. There was no hope of flooding in the natural. Therefore, no one believed Noah. But Noah believed because he could see past the natural, scientific evidence and saw what God was telling him.

Not to believe God's evidence—His word—is to believe a deception.

Noah Was Warned of God

Hebrews 11:7 says, "By faith Noah, being warned of God of things not seen as yet."

Why did God choose to warn Noah. Let's take a look at Noah's character and the issues at hand during Noah's life.

Noah's Character

Genesis 6:9 says, "These are the generations of Noah: Noah was a just man and perfect in his generations, and Noah walked with God."

Noah was a just man. What's that mean? *Just* means declared righteous. Noah was right with God because of his faith just as Abraham was. Genesis 15:6 says, "And he believed in the Lord; and he counted it to him for righteousness." When God gave warning, Noah believed Him.

Noah was a perfect man. The word *perfect* means sincere, blameless, and having integrity. Noah was a contrast to Cain. Where Cain was attempting to transform God into his image, Noah was submissive to God (as Abel was). He was sincere in his quest. Humble in obedience. Blameless in his motives. And honest with others, himself, and God. Noah didn't water down what God said or put his own interpretation on it. He just believed.

Noah was a man of good character. He was a godly man who stayed in the paths of righteousness and faith.

Abandoned Faith

Others of Noah's generation abandoned the faith handed down to them through Adam and the others mentioned in Genesis 5. Noah became the last of the godly line.

Genesis 6:5, 8 says, "And God saw that the wickedness of man was great in the earth, and that every imagination of the thoughts of his heart was only evil continually … But Noah found grace in the eyes of the Lord."

Everyone had turned from God but for a very few. Methuselah, Noah's grandfather, died shortly before the flood. Lamech, Noah's father, died the year of the flood, leaving Noah the last of a godly line. All others had apostatized. Genesis 5 is the godly line that kept the human race alive.

In his works *The Antiquities of the Jews*, Flavius Josephus has this to say of Noah's time:

> Now this posterity of Seth continued to esteem God as the Lord of the universe, and to have an entire regard to virtue, for seven generations; but in process of time they were perverted, and forsook the practices of their forefathers, and did neither pay those honours to God which were appointed them, nor had they any concern to do justice towards men. But for what degree of zeal they had formerly shewn for virtue, they now shewed by their actions a double degree of wickedness, whereby they made God to be their enemy …—
> The Works of Josephus; Antiquities of the Jews; Flavius Josephus; Chapter three, paragraph 1; Translated by William Whiston.

Men (and women) who had once followed God apostatized until there was only one left. Think of the patience that God has. He's not looking to destroy and punish, but He wants all to repent. Second Peter 3:9 says, "The Lord is not slack concerning his promise, as some men count slackness; but is longsuffering to us-ward, not willing that any should perish, but that all should come to repentance."

Sons of God

When we get into Genesis 6, we see the phrase *sons of God*. Who is the inspired writer of Genesis referring to? Angels? fallen angels? Most of the Christian community that I'm familiar with believe that these were angels that mated with women. Let's investigate and find who God was referring too. Keep in mind that God just gave us the linage of the faithful. Everyone else fell away or died by the time of the flood except Noah.

Genesis 6:1–3 says, "And it came to pass, when men began to multiply on the face of the earth, and daughters were born unto them, That the sons of God saw the daughters of men that they were fair; and they took them wives of all which they chose. And the Lord said, My spirit shall not always strive with man, for that he also is flesh: yet his days shall be an hundred and twenty years."

We'll break this down and discuss it.

Who does the Bible refer to as *not* being sons of God? The answer is the angels. Hebrews 1:5 says, "For unto which of the angels said he at any time, Thou art my Son, this day have I begotten thee?" Hebrews 1:6 then says, "And again, when he bringeth in the firstbegotten (Jesus) into the world, he saith, And let all the angels of God worship him. And of the angels he saith, Who maketh his angels spirits, and his ministers a flame of fire" (parenthesis mine). Later, Hebrews 1:13–14 says, "But to which of the angels said he at any time, Sit on my right hand, until I make thine enemies thy footstool? Are they not all ministering spirits, sent forth to minister for them who shall be heirs of salvation?"

Clearly, God has never said to any angel, "You are My Son,"

or, "Sit at My right hand." Angels are ministering spirits that do God's bidding and are sent to minister for those who will inherit salvation. They're highly skilled servants, not sons. God has never referred to angels as sons, not even in Genesis 6.

Who then are referred to as sons? The first person referred to as a son was Adam. Luke 3:38 says, "Which was the son of Enos, which was the son of Seth, which was the son of Adam, which was the son of God."

Jesus, of course, is declared the Son of God. John 1:14, 18 says, "And the Word was made flesh, and dwelt among us, (and we beheld his glory, the glory as of the only begotten of the Father,) full of grace and truth … No man hath seen God at any time; the only begotten Son, which is in the bosom of the Father, he hath declared him."

And lastly, after Jesus's resurrection, Jesus in no longer referred to as the only begotten Son of God. Those who have made Jesus Lord of their lives are called sons of God. First John 5:1 says, "Whosoever believeth that Jesus is the Christ is born of God." And 1 John 3:1–2 says, "Behold, what manner of love the Father hath bestowed upon us, that we should be called the sons of God: therefore the world knoweth us not, because it knew him not. Beloved, now are we the sons of God, and it doth not yet appear what we shall be: but we know that, when he shall appear, we shall be like him; for we shall see him as he is."

So too, if angels were referenced as being sons of God in Genesis 6, then they weren't fallen and would not have sinned by taking women as wives. The fall of Satan and his followers had taken place before this. Angels are spirit beings incapable of sexual relations with physical beings. They don't produce human seed for reproducing. They cannot create. They cannot have children.

Others have said that it was fallen angels that mated with women! How absurd. If they were fallen angels, then they wouldn't be called *sons of God*.

God blessed the union between man and woman and not interspecies propagation. Genesis 2:21–24 says,

> And the Lord God caused a deep sleep to fall upon Adam, and he slept: and he took one of his ribs, and closed up the flesh instead thereof; And the rib, which the Lord God had taken from man, made he a woman, and brought her unto the man. And Adam said, This is now bone of my bones, and flesh of my flesh: she shall be called Woman, because she was taken out of Man. Therefore shall a man leave his father and his mother, and shall cleave unto his wife: and they shall be one flesh.

(Angels don't have flesh to become one with.)

Genesis 1:27–28 says, "So God created man in his own image, in the image of God created he him; male and female created he them. And God blessed them, and God said unto them, Be fruitful, and multiply, and replenish the earth, and subdue it: and have dominion over the fish of the sea, and over the fowl of the air, and over every living thing that moveth upon the earth."

In fact, mating with anything other than the opposite sex was abominable to God. Leviticus 18:22–23 (NKJV) says, "You shall not lie with a male as with a woman. It is an abomination. Nor shall you mate with any animal, to defile yourself with it. Nor shall any woman stand before an animal to mate with it. It is perversion." Not only does God not approve of sex outside of male and female, the union doesn't produce any children. Sex with spirit beings would be the same—perversion and sterility.

In Matthew 22, Jesus said angels don't marry, indicating that they don't reproduce, and I know of nowhere in the scriptures where it says they do. God created each genus to procreate after their kind.

You may be wondering about Job's account of the sons of God. Job 1:6–7 says, "Now there was a day when the sons of God came to present themselves before the Lord, and Satan came also among them. And the Lord said unto Satan, Whence comest thou? Then Satan answered the Lord, and said, From going to and fro in the earth, and from walking up and down in it."

Who is he referring to as *sons of God*? And to whom is he not referring too? He's not referring to the angels of God. We covered this already. He's not referring to fallen angels either. Fallen angels do not present themselves to God. Nor would they be referred to as sons of God. God asked Satan where he came from. If the satanic host had presented themselves before the Lord, He wouldn't have asked.

Also, remember that God was on the outside looking into the earth. He had given dominion on the earth to Adam, who in turn gave his spiritual allegiance to Satan. Satan became Adam's new god. This is why Satan answered God the way he did. He was taunting God. He was declaring how he had bested God and could go anywhere on the earth that he wanted. The followers of God presented themselves to God, and God showed up to the presentation being held in his honor on the earth. Angels present themselves to God but not on the earth. They present themselves in heaven. Satan is on the earth, not in heaven, and he would not be able to present himself there if he even wanted to. Satan crashed the party.

So who are the sons of God in this passage? They are the godly line that came through the great flood and didn't turn from the faith. Job is thought to be the earliest written book in the Bible. It is thought to have been written during the times of the patriarchs (Abraham, Isaac, and Jacob). Shem, Noah's son, lived about fifty years after the death of Abraham. He is thought to be Melchizedek, king of Salem (later Jerusalem), priest of the Most High. He had the authority to bless Abraham. Hebrews 7:1, 4, 7 says, "For this Melchisedec, king of Salem, priest of the most high God, who met

Abraham returning from the slaughter of the kings, and blessed him ... Now consider how great this man was, unto whom even the patriarch Abraham gave the tenth of the spoils ... And without all contradiction the less is blessed of the better."

Shem headed up the godly line that came through the great flood. Because they were called sons of God before the flood, it fits that Job would continue the same phrase.

Again, we see mention to the sons of God in Job 38 when God asks Job where he was "when the morning stars sang together, and all the sons of God shouted for joy" (Job 38:4–7). This is in reference to the preflood earth. Prior to the flood, the earth was encased within "the waters which were above the firmament" (Genesis 1:7). Creation scientists' research indicates that a crystalline canopy sheltered the earth, allowing only certain light spectrums through and also acting as a type of amplifier, which allowed people to hear the sound of the stars. Preflood man would be able to hear the stars sing together.

As time passed, the sons of God fell away from the faith. What was the primary cause that the scriptures give? Genesis 6:1–3 says, "And it came to pass, when men began to multiply on the face of the earth, and daughters were born unto them, That the sons of God saw the daughters of men that they were fair; and they took them wives of all which they chose. And the Lord said, My spirit shall not always strive with man, for that he also is flesh: yet his days shall be an hundred and twenty years."

How was this important? Let's investigate another who fell into the same trap. First Kings 11:1–9 says,

> But king Solomon loved many strange women, together with the daughter of Pharaoh, women of the Moabites, Ammonites, Edomites, Zidonians, and Hittites; Of the nations concerning which the Lord said unto the children of Israel, Ye shall not go in to them, neither shall they come in unto you: for

surely they will turn away your heart after their gods: Solomon clave unto these in love. And he had seven hundred wives, princesses, and three hundred concubines: and *his wives turned away his heart*. For it came to pass, when Solomon was old, that *his wives turned away his heart after other gods*: and his heart was not perfect with the Lord his God, as was the heart of David his father. For Solomon went after Ashtoreth the goddess of the Zidonians, and after Milcom the abomination of the Ammonites. And *Solomon did evil in the sight of the Lord, and went not fully after the Lord*, as did David his father. Then did Solomon build an high place for Chemosh, the abomination of Moab, in the hill that is before Jerusalem, and for Molech, the abomination of the children of Ammon. And likewise did he for all his strange wives, which burnt incense and sacrificed unto their gods. And the Lord was angry with Solomon, because his heart was turned from the Lord God of Israel, which had appeared unto him twice. (emphasis mine)

What happened to Solomon is what happened to the sons of God in Noah's time. They married people of a different faith, and little by little, they turned from the God of Adam. Solomon was only one instance. There are many others.

We're warned of the same pitfall during our time: Second Corinthians 6:14 says, "Be ye not unequally yoked together with unbelievers: for what fellowship hath righteousness with unrighteousness? and what communion hath light with darkness?" It's the same old devil, the same old schemes.

God also said, "My Spirit shall not strive with man forever, for he is indeed flesh." God never mentioned the devil or angels or any spirit being. He's talking about men being disobedient. Genesis 6:4

says, "There were giants in the earth in those days; and also after that, when the sons of God came in unto the daughters of men, and they bare children to them, the same became mighty men which were of old, men of renown."

Of course, people have taken the word *giants* and made it into something that it isn't. The word *giants* is nephil (*Strong's Exhaustive Concordance of the Bible*) and means "prop., a *feller*, i.e. *a bully* or *tyrant: - giant.*" The center reference of my Bible says, "Heb. *Nephilim, fallen* or *mighty ones.*" It's Jewish tradition that they were the offspring of fallen angels mating with women. But when we put it in biblical perspective, they were *mighty men* who had fallen away from the faith and became tyrants. Genesis 5 and 6 were written together. They are discourse on the godly line until the last of that line—Noah. What happened to all the rest? The same thing that happened to Solomon. The blessing that God had blessed them with was turned into greed and manipulations. They became the great power brokers (bullies and tyrants) of their generations—manipulators of people, cities, and nations. They used their wealth and influence for wickedness. We see tyrants throughout history and in the earth today. Human nature has not changed.

Genesis 6:5, 11 says, "And God saw that the wickedness of man was great in the earth, and that every imagination of the thoughts of his heart was only evil continually ... The earth also was corrupt before God, and the earth was filled with violence."

This dissertation sounds like the path the world is on today. As the great schemers and power players manipulate their wills into the fabric of everyday life, fear, corruption, and violence increase. Not only the great and wealthy are corrupt. Many in the earth have turned their backs on anything to do with God. And they persecute those who want God in their lives. They devise laws that make it increasingly harder be godly while they promote everything ungodly. They use public education as a way to instill doctrines of demons in the minds of young people, and they bear false witness in the great media machine as well as tell lies and deceptions to promote their agendas. Others are using a god of violence to force their agenda in the earth. They take advantage of the moral decline of the nations and give people a false faith. With a tyrannical worldview, they bring fear, persecution, slavery, and death to all who disagree with them.

But our hope, our peace, and our security is our faith in God's word. With His word, we are to build an ark to the saving of our house.

Noah Walked with God

Noah was "perfect in his generations" (Genesis 6:9). What does that mean? It means that Noah lived by the knowledge he had. The Bible is progressive revelation, meaning that God revealed His will through the generations and not all at once. God's complete will is found in the New Testament. God's perfect will is found in Jesus. We're learning (or should be) to be like Jesus.

Amos 3:3 says, "Can two walk together, except they be agreed? God and Noah were in agreement." Noah accepted God as his God, and God accepted Noah because of his faith. Noah submitted to the known will of God, and God declared him righteous. It's the same for us. Because we accept Jesus by faith, not only does God declare us righteous, but we become righteous too. Second Corinthians 5:21 says, "For he hath made him to be sin for us, who knew no sin; that we might be made the righteousness of God in him."

God and Noah fellowshipped and communed with each other as Noah ran his life's race. Hebrews 12:1 says, "Wherefore seeing we also are compassed about with so great a cloud of witnesses (Noah being one of those witnesses), let us lay aside every weight, and the sin which doth so easily beset us, and let us run with patience the race that is set before us" (parentheses mine).

We all have a race to run. Will we walk with God? Will we lay aside "every weight, and the sin which so easily ensnares us" (NKJV) just as Noah had to do in his day? Weights aren't sins in themselves, but they hinder our fellowship with God. For instance, consider entertainment. Entertainment in itself isn't wrong. In fact, it can be healthy. But when entertainment takes us away from important time with God or keeps us from fulfilling the known will of God for our lives, then it becomes a hindrance in our lives. It becomes a weight. Plus, we have to lay aside "the sin which so easily ensnares us." A sin that can easily ensnare us is a sin that we enjoy. This sin may appear innocent to us. Sexual sins and the ease of which they are accessed are an example. For Adam and Eve, eating the forbidden fruit seemed innocent enough. Yet it was a snare. A snare isn't a trap if you can see how it works. Adam and Eve didn't see the trap for what it was. But God did. They could have avoided that trap if they would have been obedient. Every generation and every person has to choose whom they will serve, who will be their God, and what they will believe. Because sin dominated in the earth, the earth became a death trap. Noah chose to walk with God, and because of his obedience, he escaped the trap.

Before Jesus comes, there will be many snares available. When asked about His coming, the first thing Jesus said was a warning. Matthew 24:4 (NKJV) says, "And Jesus answered and said to them: 'Take heed that no one deceives you.'" The warning says, *"Don't be ensnared!"* Matthew 24 and 25 are devoted to avoiding ensnarement and the consequences of falling into the traps. Yes, Mr. and Mrs. Christian, He's talking to you.

Warned of God

It's when we're walking with God that God has our attention and can speak to us. Genesis 6:6–8, 13 says, "And it repented the Lord that he had made man on the earth, and it grieved him at his heart. And the Lord said, I will destroy man whom I have created from the face of the earth; both man, and beast, and the creeping thing, and the fowls of the air; for it repenteth me that I have made them. But Noah found grace in the eyes of the Lord. … And God said unto

Noah, The end of all flesh is come before me; for the earth is filled with violence through them."

God's will is to tell us things that we need to know and prepare for before they happen. Isaiah 42:9 says, "Behold, the former things are come to pass, and new things do I declare: before they spring forth I tell you of them." John 16:13 says, "Howbeit when he, the Spirit of truth, is come, he will guide you into all truth: for he shall not speak of himself; but whatsoever he shall hear, that shall he speak: and he will shew you things to come."

Noah was a "preacher of righteousness" (2 Peter 2:5). He was like the weatherman who foretold a coming hurricane that no one took seriously. But the storm came, and those who weren't ready were swept away. This is a sobering picture of the time before the coming of Christ. The horns blow. The announcements are made. The flags are raised, but many will not pay attention. The weathermen aren't taken seriously.

God wants us to know and prepare for things to come—not just for Christ's return but for everyday things that affect our lives. But if we're not walking with Him, how can we be available to hear from Him?

God warned Noah of things to come that had no basis in reality—the flood. Until the Ggreat flood, it had never rained on the earth. Genesis 2:5b–6 says, "For the Lord God had not caused it to rain upon the earth, and there was not a man to till the ground. But there went up a mist from the earth, and watered the whole face of the ground." God had a system to water the earth that precluded rain, storms, and hurricanes. Until Noah's flood, there hadn't been a rainbow (Genesis 9:8–17).

Human nature being what it is and unchanged through the centuries, I can imagine what people were thinking and saying. *What's rain? Where is the promise of rain? For since the fathers fell asleep, all things continue as they were from the beginning of creation.* But destruction came. Their world ended. There was no physical evidence for the coming of rain. The only evidence was God's word and Noah's actions. They had become deceived through "the lust of the flesh, the lust of the eyes, and the pride of life" (1 John 2:16). They thought they knew more than God did. After all, they had scientific proof that it couldn't rain and the earth couldn't flood. It had never happened before. They were wrong.

Take this into consideration. God was warning people, but they weren't listening. God gives the warning to the godly line of men in Genesis 5, namely those who had remained faithful from Adam to Noah. We've already read that Enoch was preaching things to come (Jude 14–15). God had been sounding the warning for many years.

Enoch's named his son Methuselah. Methuselah named his son Lamech. Lamech died the year of the flood. Lamech means destroyer. I believe that is significant. Enoch, knowing judgment was coming, passed on his faith to Methuselah. Methuselah, I believe, foresaw the destruction that was to come and named his son Lamech. Lamech named his son Noah. Noah means rest. Noah was prophesied about by his father, Lamech. Genesis 5:29 says, "And he called his name Noah, saying, This same shall comfort us concerning our work and toil of our hands, because of the ground which the Lord hath cursed."

Not unlike the deception the sons of God faced in Noah's day, the sons of God face the same today—deception in many things. People have put their hope in political parties that are corrupt and corruptible. They dream of a peaceful, better world, but it becomes more violent and disturbing. We face adversity on many fronts—foreign and domestic religious terrorism, violent gangs and organized crime, illegal aliens with greater political and legal clout than citizens, special interest groups forcing political decisions, wars, famines, nongovernmental agencies influencing or making state decisions, misinformation and disinformation propaganda, and natural disasters. But certainly, God did not tell us of the downfall of the earliest believers for naught. We have to take a stand—in love—with those whom we love and who have the greatest influence in our lives. Eve had the greatest influence in Adam's life, and he didn't stand his ground. Conversely, Adam had the greatest influence in Eve's life. What would have happened if Adam would have used that influence to help Eve defeat the temptation? We have the power of prayer, the word of God, and help from the Holy Spirit to bring our families into the will of God. As we learn to walk with God, according to His word, we'll be able to use the "weapons of our warfare" (2 Corinthians 10:3–6) more expertly, "stand against the wiles of the devil" (Ephesians 6:10–18), and pray the "effectual fervent prayer of a righteous man that avails much" (James 5:16b). We need to take the stand that Joshua did. Joshua 24:15 says, "But as for me and my house, we will serve the Lord."

All these deceptions and more (see 1 Timothy 4:1-2) combined with almost instant worldwide communication networks make for great stress in our lives. And the consequences of a stressful life are fear, violence, sickness, suicide, and every evil work. Only by walking with God can we overcome the tribulations of this world.

Noah lived in a violent world full of stress and tribulation. He and his family were alone. But God protected him and revealed His plan of redemption to him. What's God saying to His people corporately and individually during our time? It's our responsibility to make ourselves available to God to find out.

Noah took God's warning seriously. His grandfather walked with God. His father walked with God, and he walked with God. And God prepared his people for the move of God to come. So what do we know about the time of Noah? It was violent. Deception was rampant. Those who once followed God fell away. It was a time of great stress. Everyone did what was right in their own eyes. God was far from their thoughts.

But we see what God was doing as well. He protected Noah, who had stayed faithful to Him. He gave abundant opportunity for people to repent.

We see also there comes a time when God separates the believers from the unbelievers. Ezekiel 14:12–20 (NKJV) says,

The word of the LORD came again to me, saying:
"Son of man, when a land sins against Me by
persistent unfaithfulness, I will stretch out My
hand against it; I will cut off its supply of bread,
send famine on it, and cut off man and beast from
it. Even if these three men, Noah, Daniel, and Job,
were in it, they would deliver only themselves
by their righteousness," says the Lord God. "If I
cause wild beasts to pass through the land, and
they empty it, and make it so desolate that no
man may pass through because of the beasts, even
though these three men were in it, as I live," says
the Lord God, "they would deliver neither sons nor
daughters; only they would be delivered, and the
land would be desolate. Or if I bring a sword on that
land, and say, 'Sword, go through the land,' and I
cut off man and beast from it, even though these
three men were in it, as I live," says the Lord God,
"They would deliver neither sons nor daughters,
but only they themselves would be delivered. Or
if I send a pestilence into that land and pour out
my fury on it in blood, and cut off from it man and
beast, even though Noah, Daniel, and Job were in
it, as I live," says the Lord God, "they would deliver
neither son nor daughter; they would deliver only
themselves by their righteousness."

There comes a time when God has to root out the wicked in
order to save the righteous. What we see during Noah's time is
God having to cleanse the earth of the wicked in order to keep the
godly line alive. All had fallen away. Noah only remained of the
godly line. Before Jesus returns, transgressors will have "reached
their fullness" (Daniel 8:23). "And this gospel of the kingdom shall

be preached in all the world for a witness unto all nations; and then shall the end come" (Matthew 24:14).

As it was in the days of Noah, so shall it be before the coming of the Lord.

CHAPTER 4

⊷⊱⟹ ⟸⊰⊶

The Last Trumpet, the Rapture, and the Wrath of God

1 Corinthians 15:51–53

The Last Trumpet

First Corinthians 15:51-53 says, "Behold, I shew you a mystery; We shall not all sleep, but we shall all be changed, In a moment, in the twinkling of an eye, at the last trump: for the trumpet shall sound, and the dead shall be raised incorruptible, and we shall be changed. For this corruptible must put on incorruption, and this mortal must put on immortality."

This scripture says two important things that I want to emphasize. First, we *all* shall be changed at the same time. *We shall all be changed*. All declares that it happens to *everyone*, and in this scripture passage, it happens at the same time. The *all* that Paul is talking about are the *brethren* mentioned in verse 50. Obviously, he's not speaking of just the Corinthian brothers, for the rapture didn't take place during the life of the Corinthian church. No, he's talking to all those in Christ Jesus. There are those who have already gone on to be with the Lord, and some will be alive on the earth at His coming. It is at His coming when we all shall be changed.

But how can there be more than one end-time rapture if we're all changed at the same time? Well, there can't be. There are some who believe that Jesus will come and take some before the great tribulation begins and then rapture those who go through the great tribulation at the end of it. But the scripture is clear. We're all changed at the same time.

The second thing I want to emphasize is this: We all are changed at the *last trumpet*. If there is a last trumpet, then there has to be at least one other. Last means the final one. There isn't one afterward. This makes it clear that there is only one rapture.

We're all changed at the same time. The dead are raised and changed at the last trumpet, and the living are changed with the risen. We're all changed at the last trumpet.

First Thessalonians 4:15–17 says, "For this we say unto you by the word of the Lord, that we which are alive and remain unto the coming of the Lord shall not prevent them which are asleep. For the Lord himself shall descend from heaven *with a shout, with the voice of the archangel, and with the trump of God*: and the dead in Christ shall rise first: Then we which are alive and remain shall be caught up together with them in the clouds, to meet the Lord in the air: and so shall we ever be with the Lord" (emphasis mine).

When will the Lord descend from heaven? When the trumpet sounds. What trumpet? According to 1 Corinthians 15:52, it's at the *last trumpet*.

There's a shout with the voice of the Archangel. Revelation 14:15–16 says, "And another angel came out of the temple, crying with a loud voice to him that sat on the cloud, Thrust in thy sickle, and reap: for the time is come for thee to reap; for the harvest of the earth is ripe. And he that sat on the cloud thrust in his sickle on the earth; and the earth was reaped." James 5:7 says, "Be patient therefore, brethren, unto the coming of the Lord. Behold, the husbandman waiteth for the precious fruit of the earth, and hath long patience for it, until he receive the early and latter rain."

The harvest is the souls of men. When the last soul that will be saved is saved, then the harvest will come. The shout proclaims the harvest is fully ripe and ready for picking. The trumpet of God also sounds, and Jesus raises the sleeping. Then we who are alive will be caught up and meet them in the air.

The trumpet declares the triumphal entrance of the King of Kings.

The Rapture and the Wrath of God

Revelation 11:15–18 says,

> *And the seventh angel sounded;* and there were great voices in heaven, saying, *The kingdoms of this world are become the kingdoms of our Lord, and of his Christ; and he shall reign for ever and ever.* And the four and twenty elders, which sat before God on their seats, fell upon their faces, and worshipped God, Saying, We give thee thanks, O Lord God Almighty, which art, and wast, and art to come; because thou hast taken to thee thy great power, and hast reigned. And the nations were angry, and *thy wrath is come*, and the time of the dead, that they should be judged, and that thou shouldest give reward unto thy servants the prophets, and to the saints, and them that fear thy name, small and great; and shouldest destroy them which destroy the earth. (emphasis mine)

The first thing that takes place after the last trumpet sounds is the declaration, "The kingdoms of this world are become the kingdoms of our Lord, and of his Christ; and he shall reign for ever and ever."

What's happening here? The wrath of God is about to be poured out. The imminent destruction of this world order (Babylon) is upon all those on the earth, and the millennial reign of Christ is about to begin.

After this last trumpet is blown, we see that the Lord's wrath is about to be poured out. "The nations were angry, and thy wrath has come." God's wrath isn't poured out until after the last trumpet has blown—the seventh trumpet. True, before the final trumpet, there is a time of tribulation and judgment to provide an opportunity for repentance (just as Pharaoh had opportunity to repent during Moses ministry). Really, the tribulation is a time when man is reaping what he's been sowing. God is judging by taking His blessing off man's affairs. He is basically saying, "This is what you want. This is what you can have, but you won't like it. Repent, and come back to the blessing." At some point everyone has made their decision, and God calls an end to the current world order. Then Jesus will return to gather His own, and the wrath of God will be poured out upon the earth. But those who are faithful to Jesus will not be a part of the wrath.

First Thessalonians 5:9 says, "For God hath not appointed us to wrath, but to obtain salvation by our Lord Jesus Christ." At the last trumpet, we are "changed in a twinkling of an eye" (the time of the rapture), and then the wrath of God is poured out. We are not to be a part of the wrath of God, but we are a part of the great tribulation. During the great tribulation, there are souls to be saved, and we're the army of God with marching orders to preach salvation.

After reading the book of Revelation, chapters 12 through 14 seem out of play. Revelation 11 ends with the return of the Lord and the wrath of God. From Revelation 12:1 to 14:13, we have a reiteration of the tribulation period. Here's a quick outline for study:

1. Revelation 12: Satan's spiritual kingdom is overcome by the army of God (the church and the angels). This leads to Satan giving rise to the Antichrist and the abomination of desolation.
2. Revelation 13: This is what happens at the time of the abomination of desolation, including the rise of the false prophet and the mark of the Beast.

3. Revelation 14: This is an overview from the abomination of desolation to the wrath of God. The rapture occurs in verses 14–16. After the rapture (the harvest), then the wrath of God is poured out (verses 18–20).

In this outline, we again see the divine order—the great tribulation, the rapture, and then the wrath of God. Take note how Revelation 15 starts. It's in preparation for the wrath of God. Then the bowls of wrath are poured out, and the fall of Babylon is completed (Revelation 16–18). After Babylon is judged, Jesus returns with the resurrected saints, and the battle of Armageddon occurs. And finally, the millennial reign of Christ begins.

Here's another thing I want you to notice from Revelation 11. Revelation 11:18 says, "And that thou shouldest give reward unto thy servants the prophets, and to the saints, and them that fear thy name, small and great." Taken in light of what we read in Matthew (see chapter 2), it appears to me that from the time of the rapture to the battle of Armageddon, there comes the time when the saints are judged and receive their rewards. According to Jesus's teaching, He will reward the faithful upon His return.

Another interesting scripture that may or may not apply here (something to ponder) is found in Daniel 12:11–12, which says, "And from the time that the daily sacrifice shall be taken away, and the abomination that maketh desolate set up, there shall be a thousand two hundred and ninety days. Blessed is he that waiteth, and cometh to the thousand three hundred and five and thirty days." There's a forty-five-day difference. Why? What's happening during these forty-five days? Could this be the time that saints are caught up and the Beast gathers his armies to the battle of Armageddon? I think it is, but I have no definitive answer. I might be wrong, but I'm willing to learn if that's the case.

First Thessalonians 5:9 assures us that we are saved from the wrath of God. Therefore, the rapture must take place before God's wrath is poured out. But as we read the scriptures, nowhere is there a mention that we're raised before the abomination of desolation or the tribulation.

The divine order of the end times is the abomination of desolation, the great tribulation, the last trumpet, the rapture, the wrath of God, and then the millennial reign of Jesus. When we get an understanding of what to look for, we can then be better prepared for the events ahead.

CHAPTER 5

⊸⊸⊜ ⊜⊷⊷

A Look at Revelation 12–14

Revelation 12: The Leading Up to the Abomination of Desolation: Satan's Spiritual Kingdom Crashes

Second Corinthians 4:3–4 says, "But if our gospel be hid, it is hid to them that are lost: In whom the *god of this world hath blinded*" (emphasis mine).

Ephesians 6:12 (NKJV) says, "For we do not wrestle against flesh and blood, but against principalities, against powers, against the rulers of the darkness of this age, against spiritual hosts of wickedness in the *heavenly places*" (emphasis mine).

Ephesians 2:1–2 says, "And you hath he quickened, who were dead in trespasses and sins; Wherein in time past ye walked according to the course of this world, according to *the prince of the power of the air*, the spirit that now worketh in the children of disobedience" (emphasis mine).

Satan is the god of this age. He's not God. He's nowhere near God. But he is the god of the unbelieving and disobedient; hence, he's the god of this world age. Satan has blinded the minds of people for the shear enjoyment of taking them into a fiery eternity with him. He is a murderer, a thief, an accuser, and a liar. If he was human, we would say he's a psychopath, someone who has a grandiose perspective of himself, someone who does violent and

73

horrible things with great enjoyment and no remorse, and in this case, someone who is very cunning.

The devil is called the "prince of the power of the air" (Ephesians 2:2). The *air (heavenly places* in Ephesians 6:12) that Satan inhabits is the atmospheric heaven that surrounds the earth. If you read Daniel 10, you'll see that the angel sent to give Daniel understanding was withstood by "the prince of the Kingdom of Persia." This prince wasn't a physical being but a spiritual one. He was set in charge by "the prince of the power of the air" to manipulate the physical powers in Persia. Satan rules evil spirits with the intent to kill and destroy people and kingdoms.

What we see in Revelation 12 is Satan dislodged from his throne, which is in the atmospheric heaven above the earth. Jesus makes mention of this throne in Revelation 2. Revelation 2:12–13 says, "And to the angel of the church in Pergamos write; These things saith he which hath the sharp sword with two edges; I know thy works, and where thou dwellest, even where Satan's seat is."

The Covenant that Gives Birth to Jesus

Revelation 12:1–2 says, "And there appeared a great wonder in heaven; a woman clothed with the sun, and the moon under her feet, and upon her head a crown of twelve stars: And she being with child cried, travailing in birth, and pained to be delivered."

The woman mentioned here is the word of God, the covenant, and the earth that people attach their faith to. It is God's word through the ages that gave birth to Jesus in the earth. It is the faith of those of the covenants. It is everyone who believed God would send the Messiah. Jesus is the Word of God made flesh (John 1:14). It is Adam, Abel, Seth, Enoch, Noah, Abraham, Moses, and others who received the word of God in faith and made way for Jesus to be born. The people of Israel, of course, became a part of that covenant. The twelve stars represent the twelve tribes. The woman is clothed with the sun. She's been the bright light of the ages that has brought hope to a dark world. She is the glory of God. What illuminates all of history is the Word of God. The woman is God's word to man.

The moon is the Law. The brightness of the moon is a reflection of the glory of the sun. It is the woman that shines like the sun, and the moon is a reflection of the sun. The good things of the New Testament ratified by Christ's blood (Hebrews 8:6) were shadows in the law (Hebrews 10:1). Have you noticed that the moon is only mentioned once in connection to the woman? But Jesus and those who keep the commandments of God and have the testimony of Jesus Christ are mentioned as being the woman's offspring (Revelation 12:17).

Notice what Paul wrote to the Galatians. Galatians 4:21–26, 28 says,

> Tell me, ye that desire to be under the law, do ye not hear the law? For it is written, that Abraham had two sons, the one by a bondmaid, the other by a freewoman. But he who was of the bondwoman was born after the flesh; but he of the freewoman was by promise. Which things are an allegory: for these are the two covenants; the one from the mount Sinai, which gendereth to bondage, which is Agar. For this Agar is mount Sinai in Arabia, and answereth to Jerusalem which now is, and is in bondage with her children. But Jerusalem which is above is free, which is the *mother of us all* ... Now we, brethren, as Isaac was, are the *children of promise*. (emphasis mine)

You see, the *mother* of us all is the word of God—the word of faith. The *mother* cried out in labor to give birth to a new creation, a new covenant in Christ Jesus (2 Corinthians 5:17). People are still brought into the kingdom of God through the labor and pain of the praying saint.

Isaiah 66:7–9 says,

> Before she travailed, she brought forth; before
> her pain came, she was delivered of a man child.
> Who hath heard such a thing? who hath seen such
> things? Shall the earth be made to bring forth
> in one day? or shall a nation be born at once? for
> as soon as Zion travailed, she brought forth her
> children. Shall I bring to the birth, and not cause
> to bring forth? saith the Lord: shall I cause to bring
> forth, and shut the womb? saith thy God.

No one has ever heard of a child being born before the pain
of labor. Nations aren't sudden happenings. No, it takes work.
And today's sacrifices are tomorrow's blessings. The same is true
spiritually. Most of us have had the idea that somehow God just
coaxes people into His kingdom without any real plan or design. But
it takes labor. It takes the labor, pain, inconvenience, sacrifice, and
work of saints witnessing, supporting God's ministries, studying
the Word, and laboring in prayer.

Galatians 4:19 says, "My little children, of whom I travail in
birth again until Christ be formed in you." Paul said that he labored
in birth *again. Again?* Yes, he labored originally so that Zion would
give to her children. And now he's laboring again so that they may
grow up spiritually. This is God's method of bringing children into
the kingdom of God. How was He laboring?

Colossians 4:12–13 says, "Epaphras, who is one of you, a servant
of Christ, saluteth you, always labouring fervently for you in prayers,
that ye may stand perfect and complete in all the will of God. For
I bear him record, that he hath a great zeal for you, and them that
are in Laodicea, and them in Hierapolis." How did Epaphras labor?
In prayer. He was praying so that they would "stand perfect and
complete in all the will of God."

How do we pray when we know we need to pray but don't

know exactly what to pray for? Both Paul and Epaphras knew that these Christians needed to grow up spiritually and be in God's will, but how could they know with confidence that they were praying effectively?

Romans 8:26 says, "Likewise the Spirit also helpeth our infirmities: for we know not what we should pray for as we ought: but the Spirit itself maketh intercession for us with groanings which cannot be uttered."

I can appreciate the Amplified Bible's version of this scripture. Romans 8:26 (AMP) says, "So too the [Holy] Spirit comes to our aid and bears us up in our weakness; for we do not know what prayer to offer nor how to offer it worthily as we ought, but the Spirit Himself goes to meet our supplication and pleads in our behalf with unspeakable yearnings and groanings too deep for utterance."

It's important to take note that the Holy Spirit comes "to meet out supplication." In other words, we're praying, and as we're praying, He comes along side to help. Why do we need Him to help us? We're praying about something, and we may not understand how to pray effectively about it. We have a "weakness: for we do not know what prayer to offer nor how to offer it worthily as we ought."

These scripture passages help to explain the one we just read in Romans. First Corinthians 14:2, 14 says, "For he that speaketh in an unknown tongue speaketh not unto men, but unto God: for no man understandeth him; howbeit in the spirit he speaketh mysteries ... For if I pray in an unknown tongue, my spirit prayeth, but my understanding is unfruitful."

You see? Praying in tongues is praying in the spirit. It is the Holy Spirit helping our spirit pray. And praying in the spirit is praying out the *mysteries* of God. In other words, the Spirit is coming to our aid to help in our *weaknesses*.

In Romans, Paul mentions the Spirit helping us with "unspeakable yearnings and groanings too deep for utterance." There's a place in prayer that goes beyond words, a place of labor and birth pangs. God labored in birth pangs until Jesus was manifested in the earth. We continue with Him so others can be born into the kingdom of God. Revivals are birth through the labor and pain of the saints.

Satan Kicked Out of Heaven

Revelation 12:3–4 says, "And there appeared another wonder in heaven; and behold a great red dragon, having seven heads and ten horns, and seven crowns upon his heads. And his tail drew the third part of the stars of heaven, and did cast them to the earth."

These verses describe the fall of Lucifer to the earth when he rebelled against God. Bible scholars believe that Satan caused a third of the heavenly host to fall with him in his rebellion. God didn't have any problem disposing of Satan. Jesus described Satan's exile from heaven to happen as fast as lightning (Luke 10:18).

Jesus Is Born

Revelation 12:4–6 says,

> And his tail drew the third part of the stars of heaven, and did cast them to the earth: and the dragon stood before the woman which was ready to be delivered, for to devour her child as soon as it was born. And she brought forth a man child, who was to rule all nations with a rod of iron: and her child was caught up unto God, and to his throne. And the woman fled into the wilderness, where she hath a place prepared of God, that they should feed her there a thousand two hundred and threescore days.

Ever since the fall of Adam, Satan has been waiting for the promised Messiah. Satan's goal has always been to destroy the

Messiah as soon as He was born. Remember when Jesus was born and King Herod had all the male children two years old and younger murdered (Matthew 2:16–18)? But Jesus was born in spite of Satan's efforts to the contrary. And now Jesus sits at the right hand of God (Hebrews 1:13; 10:12). He is destined to rule all nations on the earth (Revelation 2:26–27; 20:4–6). The woman is the people of the covenant, the children of promise, Jesus being the firstborn (Romans 8.29; Colossians 1:15, 18; Revelation 1:5).

Take note of how long the woman flees into the wilderness. It is an important time frame—1,260 days. This is the amount of time of the great tribulation, ending with the wrath of God being poured out. This places us in the period of the end of the end times.

The Prince of the Power of the Air (Satan) Is Cast Out of the Atmospheric Heavens

Revelation 12:7–12 says,

> And there was war in heaven: Michael and his angels fought against the dragon; and the dragon fought and his angels, And prevailed not; neither was their place found any more in heaven. And the great dragon was cast out, that old serpent, called the Devil, and Satan, which deceiveth the whole world: he was cast out into the earth, and his angels were cast out with him.
>
> And I heard a loud voice saying in heaven, Now is come salvation, and strength, and the kingdom of our God, and the power of his Christ: for the accuser of our brethren is cast down, which accused them before our God day and night. And they overcame him by the blood of the Lamb, and by the word of their testimony; and they loved not their lives unto the death. Therefore rejoice,

ye heavens, and ye that dwell in them. Woe to the inhabiters of the earth and of the sea! for the devil is come down unto you, having great wrath, because he knoweth that he hath but a short time.

War broke out in heaven. This isn't speaking of the time Satan was cast out of God's heaven after he rebelled. During this war Satan's wrath will be manifested to the "inhabitants of the earth and sea." This is describing the events that led up to the abomination of desolation. Satan is overthrown from his earthly, atmospheric position, and *he knows that he has a short time.*

Satan's spiritual kingdom collapses—that is, he's cast down from his throne. His only recourse is to get behind an individual on earth (the Antichrist). Then the kingdoms of men, manifested as Babylon, the great harlot, will collapse. In these scripture passages, we see Satan fall from his spiritual throne and have to take up a throne through a man. In Revelation 19, we see the kingdom of Babylon collapse and Jesus rule over the kingdoms of men.

Revelation 19:11–16 says,

> And I saw heaven opened, and behold a white horse; and he that sat upon him was called Faithful and True, and in righteousness he doth judge and make war. His eyes were as a flame of fire, and on his head were many crowns; and he had a name written, that no man knew, but he himself. And he was clothed with a vesture dipped in blood: and his name is called The Word of God. And the armies which were in heaven followed him upon white horses, clothed in fine linen, white and clean. And out of his mouth goeth a sharp sword, that with it he should smite the nations: and he shall rule them with a rod of iron: and he treadeth the winepress of the fierceness and wrath of Almighty God. And

he hath on his vesture and on his thigh a name
written, King of Kings, and Lord of Lords.

Notice what is said after Satan is cast out of heaven. Revelation
12:10 says, "And I heard a loud voice saying in heaven, Now is
come salvation, and strength, and the kingdom of our God, and
the power of his Christ: for the accuser of our brethren is cast
down, which accused them before our God day and night." This
is the event that precipitates the abomination of desolation. This
is Satan's final thrust for destroying the earth's inhabitants. When
Satan first rebelled against God, the Christ had yet to come. The
Christ has come in this scripture. Moreover, at that time of the
devil's initial rebellion, the kingdom of God didn't have to come. It
already exited. Furthermore, "they overcame him by the blood of
the Lamb and by the word of their testimony, and they loved not
their lives unto the death," firmly establishes this time during the
church age.

I find it interesting that this event occurs at a time when the
saints of God "overcame him by the blood of the Lamb, and by
the word of their testimony; and they loved not their lives unto
the death." This isn't a weak church. This describes an army of
believers that will do and say what the Lord of the Host of God says,
even if that means sacrificing their lives! Wow! We enjoy quoting
the first part of that verse, but few have quoted the last part. You
should read the book of Joel. He describes the army of the Lord in
the lasts days.

Daniel 12 describes this event. Daniel 12:1–3 says,

> And at that time shall Michael stand up, the great
> prince which standeth for the children of thy
> people: *and there shall be a time of trouble, such as
> never was since there was a nation even to that same
> time*: and at that time thy people shall be delivered,
> every one that shall be found written in the book.

> And many of them that sleep in the dust of the earth shall awake, some to everlasting life, and some to shame and everlasting contempt. And they that be wise shall shine as the brightness of the firmament; and they that turn many to righteousness as the stars for ever and ever. (emphasis mine)

It is when Satan is cast out of his heavenly realm that the great tribulation ("a time of trouble, such as never was since there was a nation, even to that same time") begins to take form. Then the Antichrist rises to power, and the end of the age is in its final time. I believe what causes Satan to crash is the faith of the faithful and divine providence.

Revelation 12:11 says, "And they overcame him by the blood of the Lamb, and by the word of their testimony; and they loved not their lives unto the death." James 5:7–8 says, "Be patient therefore, brethren, unto the coming of the Lord. Behold, the husbandman waiteth for the precious fruit of the earth, and hath long patience for it, until he receive the early and latter rain. Be ye also patient; stablish your hearts: for the coming of the Lord draweth nigh." Matthew 24:14 says, "And this gospel of the kingdom shall be preached in all the world for a witness unto all nations; and then shall the end come."

Jesus comes at the appointed time of the Father. I believe, as we just read, that part of the plan of God is the maturity and faithfulness of the saints that causes the gospel to be preached effectively in the most trying time in earth's history. The "gospel of the kingdom will be preached in all the world" by a strong body of believers. Therefore, Satan attempts to destroy the church like he never has before. He's unsuccessful, and then he must share his power as he never has before. Satan is very selfish and doesn't share. He's a liar, a thief, and a murderer. He will offer the foolish power but only a little and always with the intent to control and destroy. Those who are involved in magic, clairvoyance, and other occult practices will find in death that they have fallen prey to the psychopath of psychopaths and that they will not sit with Satan on his throne or share his power. The only thing that they will share in is the lake of fire.

Yet in a last-ditch effort, Satan brings together all his influence and power to deceive the nations and kill the Christians with the intent to buy more time. In doing so, he predominately throws his forces behind one man—the Antichrist.

The Dragon, the Woman, and the Rest

The Dragon

The dragon persecutes the woman who flees into the wilderness "for a time, and times, and half a time" (Revelation 12:14) or 1,260 days (Revelation 12:6). The serpent doesn't succeed in killing the woman. Revelation 12:13–16 says,

> And when the dragon saw that he was cast unto the earth, he persecuted the woman which brought forth the man child. And to the woman were given two wings of a great eagle, that she might fly into the wilderness, into her place, where she is nourished for a time, and times, and half a time, from the face of the serpent. And the serpent cast out of his mouth water as a flood after the woman, that he might cause her to be carried away of the flood. And the earth helped the woman, and the earth opened her mouth, and swallowed up the flood which the dragon cast out of his mouth.

As I made mention before, the woman is the people of the covenant. When Satan is cast down, who does he go after? He goes after the people of the covenant. But the covenant people are protected, even though they are in the wilderness, for "the earth helped the woman, and the earth opened her mouth, and swallowed up the flood which the dragon cast out of his mouth."

A Word on the Wilderness

The wilderness is not the rapture, heaven, or any such place. Heaven is not a wilderness that we escape to. Paul called heaven paradise (2 Corinthians 12:3–4). Noah escaped in an ark. He was *in* the world but not *of* the world. The ark was not a paradise. It was more like a wilderness. It was a place of safety in a time of tribulation.

What does the scripture say concerning John the Baptist? Matthew 3:1–3 says, "In those days came John the Baptist, preaching in the wilderness of Judaea, And saying, Repent ye: for the kingdom of heaven is at hand. For this is he that was spoken of by the prophet Esaias, saying, The voice of one crying in the wilderness, Prepare ye the way of the Lord, make his paths straight."

What do we see about John? He was in the wilderness. He was preaching. His topic was as follows: "Repent, for the kingdom of heaven is at hand. Prepare the way of the Lord; Make his paths straight."

What will the church do before the coming of the Lord? We will be preaching the gospel to all nations to gather the precious fruit of the earth. We will be preaching, "Repent, for the kingdom of heaven is at hand. Prepare the way of the Lord Jesus."

Will we be doing this from heaven? No. Isaiah 40:3–5 says, "The voice of him that crieth in the wilderness, Prepare ye the way of the Lord, make straight in the desert a highway for our God. Every valley shall be exalted, and every mountain and hill shall be made low: and the crooked shall be made straight, and the rough places plain: And the glory of the Lord shall be revealed, and all flesh shall see it together: for the mouth of the Lord hath spoken it."

The phrase "Make straight in the desert a highway for our God" doesn't give the appearance of heaven but of a sinful earth.

And the expression "The glory of the LORD shall be revealed, and all flesh shall see it together" certainly concerns this sin-filled earth.

The earth is the wilderness. As we approach the coming of our Savior, the more chaotic and desolate it will become. This will become a breeding ground for every cultic, demonic spirit to entice people to accept the antithesis of the Savior—someone who gives the appearance of a savior but who in reality leads into eternal prison. People everywhere will have the opportunity to choose which savior they will make Lord.

Time and Times and Half a Time

"Time and times and half a time" refers to the great tribulation period. This is in reference to the time after the Antichrist has set up the abomination of desolation and spans until sin has reached its fullness. It's three and a half years. Remember what Jesus said in Matthew 24? "Therefore when you see the 'abomination of desolation' … then there will be great tribulation." This coincides with the 1,260 days that the woman is in the wilderness (Revelation 12:6).

The Rest

Revelation 12:17 says, "And the dragon was wroth with the woman, and went to make war with the remnant of her seed, which keep the commandments of God, and have the testimony of Jesus Christ."

Who are the *rest of her offspring*? They are those *who keep the commandments of God and have the testimony of Jesus Christ*. The offspring and the *rest* of the woman's offspring are Christians. The physical Jews are not the offspring. Let me give you some scripture passages so that you understand why I say this.

Romans 9:1–8 says,

> I say the truth in Christ, I lie not, my conscience also bearing me witness in the Holy Ghost, That I have

great heaviness and continual sorrow in my heart. For I could wish that myself were accursed from Christ for my brethren, my kinsmen according to the flesh: Who are Israelites; to whom pertaineth the adoption, and the glory, and the covenants, and the giving of the law, and the service of God, and the promises; Whose are the fathers, and of whom as concerning the flesh Christ came, who is over all, God blessed for ever. Amen.

Not as though the word of God hath taken none effect. *For they are not all Israel, which are of Israel: Neither, because they are the seed of Abraham, are they all children: but, In Isaac shall thy seed be called. That is, They which are the children of the flesh, these are not the children of God: but the children of the promise are counted for the seed.* (emphasis mine)

You see, Abraham had two sons one from Hagar (Ishmael) and one from Sarah (Isaac). Ishmael was conceived by natural ways. That is, there was no supernatural intervention. There was no faith, only a man and woman who had a child.

On the other hand, Isaac was born by supernatural intervention. Isaac was promised by God. Abraham and Sarah believed God's word, and Isaac was born. Abraham was a hundred years old, and Sarah was ninety years old when Isaac was born, well past the age of childbearing. Isaac was a supernaturally born son because God had made a promise.

Now what Paul is saying is that God's children aren't those who are born from Abraham by natural means but by supernatural means. God's children are those who have taken the promise in faith. Romans 9:30–33 says,

What shall we say then? That the Gentiles, which followed not after righteousness, have attained to righteousness, even the righteousness which is of faith. But Israel, which followed after the law of righteousness, hath not attained to the law of righteousness. Wherefore? Because they sought it not by faith, but as it were by the works of the law. For they stumbled at that stumblingstone; As it is written, Behold, I lay in Sion a stumblingstone and rock of offence: and whosoever believeth on him shall not be ashamed.

What is the promise that we must take by faith? "Whosoever believeth on Him will not be put to shame." Whoever believes on Jesus is a child of promise by faith.

Galatians 3:6–9 says, "Even as Abraham believed God, and it was accounted to him for righteousness. Know ye therefore that they which are of faith, the same are the children of Abraham. And the scripture, foreseeing that God would justify the heathen through faith, preached before the gospel unto Abraham, saying, In thee shall all nations be blessed. So then they which be of faith are blessed with faithful Abraham."

Galatians 4:22–25, 28 says,

> For it is written, that Abraham had two sons, the one by a bondmaid, the other by a freewoman. But he who was of the bondwoman was born after the flesh; but he of the freewoman was by promise. Which things are an allegory: for these are the two covenants; the one from the mount Sinai, which gendereth to bondage, which is Agar. For this Agar is mount Sinai in Arabia, and answereth to Jerusalem which now is, and is in bondage with her children ... Now we, brethren, as Isaac was, are the children of promise.

Who are the children of promise? Those of us in the new covenant.

Who is Satan out to make war with? Those who have caused his last days. Those who have the testimony of Jesus Christ. Those of the faith of Abraham.

It also seems to me that there will be Christians who will get into the army of God only when they see the abomination of desolation. Then they'll realize that they're risking eternity if they don't get their lives moving in the right direction.

Daniel relates this in this scripture and seems to parallel what John wrote concerning the "rest of her offspring, who keep the commandments of God and have the testimony of Jesus Christ" (Revelation 12:17).

Daniel 11:32-35 says,

> And such as do wickedly against the covenant shall he corrupt by flatteries: but the people that do know their God shall be strong, and do exploits. And they that understand among the people shall instruct many: yet they shall fall by the sword, and by flame, by captivity, and by spoil, many days. Now when they shall fall, they shall be holpen with a little help: but many shall cleave to them with flatteries. *And some of them of understanding shall fall, to try them, and to purge, and to make them white, even to the time of the end*: because it is yet for a time appointed. (emphasis mine)

There will be those who have joined in the army of the Lord and will be strong and will carry out great exploits in the name of Jesus. They will bring many into the kingdom of God during that time. But there are those who have the testimony of Jesus but have never joined the army of Jesus. "And some of them of understanding shall fall, to try them, and to purge, and to make them white, even to the time of the end." I think that some are going to get their act together just before it's too late. I say I think this will happen because this is just my opinion, but the scriptures seem to point in that direction. The parable of the ten virgins makes it clear that there are those who have the oil and make it and those who should have the oil and don't make it (Matthew 25:1–13). Some will awake to righteousness just in time.

Revelation 13: What Happens at the Time of the Abomination of Desolation?

Revelation 13:1–8 says,

> And I stood upon the sand of the sea, and saw a beast rise up out of the sea, having seven heads and ten horns, and upon his horns ten crowns, and upon his heads the name of blasphemy. And the beast which I saw was like unto a leopard, and his feet were as the feet of a bear, and his mouth as the mouth of a lion: and the dragon gave him his power, and his seat, and great authority. And I saw one of his heads as it were wounded to death; and his deadly wound was healed: and all the world wondered after the beast. And they worshipped the dragon which gave power unto the beast: and they worshipped the beast, saying, Who is like unto the beast? who is able to make war with him? And there was given unto him a mouth speaking great things and blasphemies; and power was given unto him to continue forty and two months. And he opened his mouth in blasphemy against God, to blaspheme his name, and his tabernacle, and them that dwell in heaven. And it was given unto him to make war with the saints, and to overcome

them: and power was given him over all kindreds, and tongues, and nations. And all that dwell upon the earth shall worship him, whose names are not written in the book of life of the Lamb slain from the foundation of the world.

Satan is enraged, and he goes off to make war with those who keep the commandments of God and have the testimony of Jesus Christ. In chapter 13, we see the Beast (or Antichrist) rise to power. This power comes from the Dragon (Satan). Satan gives the Antichrist "his power, his throne, and great authority," as we see in verses 2 and 4.

Satan Gives His Power and Authority to the Antichrist

Revelation 13:2, 4 says, "And the beast which I saw was like unto a leopard, and his feet were as the feet of a bear, and his mouth as the mouth of a lion: and the dragon gave him his power, and his seat, and great authority ... And they worshipped the dragon which gave power unto the beast: and they worshipped the beast, saying, Who is like unto the beast? who is able to make war with him?"

The Beast is Satan's answer to his predicament because his time is short. Satan's problem is God's appointed time has come and a successful and faithful church has established herself in the earth. Therefore, he intends to kill as many Christians and take as many unbelievers to hell with him as he can before he's chained and imprisoned in the abyss. His answer is to entice the nations under the leadership of the Beast. Satan isn't trying to save the planet and its people. He isn't trying to end world hunger, war, and disease. He couldn't if he wanted to. He's nothing but a murderer, thief, and destroyer (John 10:10). His only aim is to throw as many assailants against the church as possible.

I want to make Revelation 13:7 clear. Verse 7 isn't telling us that God is granting permission for the Beast to make war with the saints. Don't let the Deceiver put that into your thoughts. Revelation 13:7 actually says, "And it was given unto him to make war with the saints, and to overcome them: and power was given him over all kindreds, and tongues, and nations."

Who then is giving the Antichrist this authority? It's the leaders of the nations that are worshipping him. In verses 4 through 6, we see that the Beast is worshipped. The nations' god, the Beast, preaches against the God of heaven and those who worship the God of heaven. Who do you think that his followers will want to kill? Every last Christian that they can find—that's who.

This isn't new thinking. Hitler insisted that Jews should be killed even when he knew that his days were numbered. Pharaoh's heart was so hardened and his followers so loyal that even when God's power was overwhelmingly displayed, they refused to yield to the Lord. They rebelled even to the point of following the Israelites into the sea to their deaths.

The Beast Continues for Forty-two Months and Wars with the Saints

Verses 5 through 8 contain the forty-two months of the great tribulation. Transgression is at an all-time peak at this time.

Revelation 13:5 says, "And there was given unto him a mouth speaking great things and blasphemies; and power was given unto him to continue forty and two months." Daniel 8:23–26 (NKJV) says,

> And in the latter time of their kingdom, *when the transgressors have reached their fullness,* A king shall arise, having fierce features, who understands sinister schemes. His power shall be mighty, but not by his own power; he shall destroy fearfully, and shall destroy the mighty, and also the holy people. Through his cunning he shall cause

deceit to prosper under his rule; and he shall exalt himself in his heart. He shall destroy many in their prosperity. He shall even rise against the Prince of princes; but he shall be broken without human means. And the vision of the evenings and mornings which was told is true; therefore seal up the vision, for it refers to many days in the future. (emphasis mine)

The earth is full. There are no more oceans to cross to a new land. There are no open and uncharted lands to find. Stress and pressure in the earth is contained in the earth. The earth is a pressure cooker. There is no relief valve. What happens on one side of the earth is known within hours on the other side. This pressure will keep building until some will do anything for relief, including believing a lie and worshipping Satan. As Hitler blamed the Jews for Germany's troubles and Nero blamed the Christians for Rome's problems, so the Antichrist turns the world against Christians. Propaganda, disinformation, war, murder, and every evil work are in his arsenal. He continues for forty-two months and is then destroyed by the Lord of Hosts, Jesus Christ. It's not that his sinister schemes aren't in operation before the forty-two months start, because they certainly are, but we see the results of his scheming at the start of the forty-two months. Those who are already corrupt and involved in sinister schemes are the ones first involved in the "one world order" war. World bankers, world terrorist leaders, world politicians, and world business leaders will be involved. People with the knowledge of the inner workings of the world systems and how to manipulate those systems to their advantage will also play roles. His move for world domination brings about the abomination of desolation and the forced worship of himself as deity. I won't get into it now, but Revelation 6:2 is the start of the Antichrist's move for world domination as well as the cause (and the beginning) of the great tribulation. We know this by the opening of the other seals. The Antichrist's reign of terror lasts forty-two months, and then he is cast into the lake of fire forever.

Let's look at the warning in verses 9 and 10.

Faith and Patience in the Tribulation

Revelation 13:9–10 says, "If any man have an ear, let him hear. He that leadeth into captivity shall go into captivity: he that killeth with the sword must be killed with the sword. Here is the patience and the faith of the saints."

Why does he say that this is the patience and the faith of the saints? He's saying we're going to have to endure this and keep the faith until this runs its course and is over. There's going to be deception. There's going to be murder and persecution.

This is the patience of the saints—patience not to be led into captivity by receiving the mark of the Beast or following deceptive practices. In the gospels, Jesus's first remarks about His return include a warning not to be deceived by false Christs and prophets. Do not forget this. Receiving the mark of the Beast is a guarantee to eternal punishment.

Revelation 14:9–12 says,

> And the third angel followed them, saying with a loud voice, If any man worship the beast and his image, and receive his mark in his forehead, or in his hand, The same shall drink of the wine of the wrath of God, which is poured out without mixture into the cup of his indignation; and he shall be tormented with fire and brimstone in the presence of the holy angels, and in the presence of the Lamb: And the smoke of their torment ascendeth up for ever and ever: and they have no rest day nor night, who worship the beast and his image, and whosoever receiveth the mark of his

name. Here is the patience of the saints: here are
they that keep the commandments of God, and the
faith of Jesus.

You need to understand that the Beast intends to control
religion, politics, and the economy. He'll come in and promise
peace and prosperity if the world will worship him. Of course,
believers will not worship him, and this gives him power by the
nations to kill Christians. The temptations will be great to receive
the mark of the Beast. Some will say, "God will forgive me. He
knows that we have to eat. He'll understand that I have to take
care of my children." But there will be no forgiveness. And those
who worship the Beast and his image are forever lost. If you'll
read the book of Hebrews, you'll understand that it was written
to encourage Christians not to fall back into perdition by denying
Christ. They were tempted to do so because of persecution.

This leads us to the faith of the saints. Jesus asked, "When the
Son of man comes, will he really find faith on the earth?" (Luke
18:8). It's our faith that overcomes the world (1 John 5:4). It's our faith
that receives from God (Mark 11:24). It's our faith that gives us a
good report with God (Hebrews 11). We need to develop our faith
now while it is *easy* and not be unprepared for the time to come.
It's important that we realize that God is our salvation and that He
will never leave us or forsake us in spite of the circumstances. It is
important to know in our hearts that God is the answer and not
the problem.

The False Prophet

Revelation 13:11–13 says, "And I beheld another beast coming up
out of the earth; and he had two horns like a lamb, and he spake
as a dragon. And he exerciseth all the power of the first beast
before him, and causeth the earth and them which dwell therein
to worship the first beast, whose deadly wound was healed. And

he doeth great wonders, so that he maketh fire come down from heaven on the earth in the sight of men."

Here we see a second beast. We'll call him the false prophet because he can do nothing outside the presence of the Antichrist. In the presence of the Antichrist, the false prophet does signs and wonders. In Matthew 24:24, Jesus said, "For there shall arise false Christs, and false prophets, and shall shew great signs and wonders; insomuch that, if it were possible, they shall deceive the very elect."

The false prophet causes an image to be made of the Beast. Then he even causes the image to speak. And he puts to death those who will not worship the Beast and the image. Jesus warns His people not to be deceived. Stay faithful to the word of God.

The Abomination of Desolation

Revelation 13:15–18 says,

> And he had power to give life unto the image of the beast, that the image of the beast should both speak, and cause that as many as would not worship the image of the beast should be killed. And he causeth all, both small and great, rich and poor, free and bond, to receive a mark in their right hand, or in their foreheads: And that no man might buy or sell, save he that had the mark, or the name of the beast, or the number of his name. Here is wisdom. Let him that hath understanding count the number of the beast: for it is the number of a man; and his number is Six hundred threescore and six.

The making of the image, its subsequent speaking, and the worship of it is the abomination of desolation. This is the beginning of the final three and a half years of this age. It is the beginning of the great tribulation.

Matthew 24:15, 21–22 says, "When ye therefore shall see the abomination of desolation, spoken of by Daniel the prophet, stand in the holy place, (whoso readeth, let him understand:) ... For then shall be great tribulation, such as was not since the beginning of the world to this time, no, nor ever shall be. And except those days should be shortened, there should no flesh be saved: but for the elect's sake those days shall be shortened." Daniel 12:11 says, "And from the time that the daily sacrifice shall be taken away, and the abomination that maketh desolate set up, there shall be a thousand two hundred and ninety days."

I want you to take note that the mark of the Beast doesn't occur until after the abomination of desolation is set up (Revelation 13:15–18). Taking the mark, name, or number of the Beast indicates that you have made him your god. In effect, it is the mark of the covenant between the Beast and those who choose him as god. It says that you trust him to supply your every need.

The oracle writes, "Here is wisdom." Wisdom is skill in life and the ability to foresee the consequence of action. He didn't say, "Here is understanding of the reason for this number." He who accepts this number, name, or mark will know that this is the Antichrist, and whoever receives this number is doomed to eternal torment.

Revelation 14: Overview from the Abomination of Desolation to the Wrath of God

The 144,000

Revelation 14:1–5 says,

> And I looked, and, lo, a Lamb stood on the mount Sion, and with him an hundred forty and four thousand, having his Father's name written in their foreheads. And I heard a voice from heaven, as the voice of many waters, and as the voice of a great

thunder: and I heard the voice of harpers harping with their harps: And they sung as it were a new song before the throne, and before the four beasts, and the elders: and no man could learn that song but the hundred and forty and four thousand, which were redeemed from the earth. These are they which were not defiled with women; for they are virgins. These are they which follow the Lamb whithersoever he goeth. These were redeemed from among men, being the firstfruits unto God and to the Lamb. And in their mouth was found no guile: for they are without fault before the throne of God.

This appears to be taking place at the sealing of the 144,000 after the abomination of desolation in Revelation 7:4–8. These are redeemed Jews who will give testimony of Jesus during the great tribulation. I have no insight on this.

Preaching in the Great Tribulation

During the great tribulation, the gospel will still be preached. The question is this: Who will be preaching it? Will it be an angel? Will it be the church? Revelation 14:6–11 says,

And I saw another angel fly in the midst of heaven, having the everlasting gospel to preach unto them that dwell on the earth, and to every nation, and kindred, and tongue, and people, Saying with a loud voice, Fear God, and give glory to him; for the hour of his judgment is come: and worship him that made heaven, and earth, and the sea, and the fountains of waters.

And there followed another angel, saying, Babylon is fallen, is fallen, that great city, because

> she made all nations drink of the wine of the wrath of her fornication.
>
> And the third angel followed them, saying with a loud voice, If any man worship the beast and his image, and receive his mark in his forehead, or in his hand, The same shall drink of the wine of the wrath of God, which is poured out without mixture into the cup of his indignation; and he shall be tormented with fire and brimstone in the presence of the holy angels, and in the presence of the Lamb: And the smoke of their torment ascendeth up for ever and ever: and they have no rest day nor night, who worship the beast and his image, and whosoever receiveth the mark of his name.

We can see here angels declaring the gospel, so we know that angels have something to do with the spreading of God's word. But what is their part? Angels are responsible for delivering the Word to those who preach it. Take a look. Galatians 3:19 (NKJV) says, "What purpose then does the law serve? It was added because of transgressions, till the Seed should come to whom the promise was made; *and it was appointed through angels by the hand of a mediator*" (emphasis mine). And Hebrews 2:1–2 says, "Therefore we ought to give the more earnest heed to the things which we have heard, lest at any time we should let them slip. *For if the word spoken by angels was stedfast*, and every transgression and disobedience received a just recompence of reward" (emphasis mine).

We can see all through the scriptures that God sends His word forth by angels and that men declare it. Read Daniel 4. Nebuchadnezzar was given a dream in which an angel declared to him things that were going to take place. It was Daniel that declared the interpretation. In the first chapters of Revelation, we see Jesus saying, "To the angel of the church of … write." Angels have a place, and people have a place. I believe that what is happening in Revelation 14 is what is principally preached during the great tribulation. For instance, consider Revelation 14:6–7, which says, "And I saw another angel fly in the midst of heaven, having the everlasting gospel to preach unto them that dwell on the earth, and to every nation, and kindred, and tongue, and people, Saying with a loud voice, Fear God, and give glory to him; for the hour of his judgment is come: and worship him that made heaven, and earth, and the sea, and the fountains of waters."

Sure, an angel is delivering the message, but it has always been the church that is to take it to mankind. Jesus told the church to go preach the gospel. Does it make any sense that a lone angel is circling the earth declaring this message? Who would lead anyone to Christ? Will the angel give altar calls? Will he lay hands on the sick? When would he have time?

The angels are delivering spiritual messages that the church will deliver physically. What's the first angel delivering? He's declaring that God's judgment is coming, so he beckons us to worship God and stop worshipping other things.

A time is coming when judgment will come. But God wants repentance, not judgment. He says, "Come! And let him who hears say, Come! And let him who thirsts come. Whoever desires let him take the water of life freely" (Revelation 22:17 NKJV). This is the last opportunity to accept God's gift of Jesus.

I've got news for you! God is not pulling His army out at the last minute and letting the world die. He's keeping His army in the fight until those days have to be shortened or *no* flesh would survive, but for the elects' sake, those days will be shortened (Matthew 24:22). God is going to rescue everyone that will accept Jesus, and the only ones left on the earth when Jesus takes us away will be those who have willfully chosen not to worship God.

So it seems to me that this gospel will be preached in all the earth. What will be preached?

1. The first angel says, "Worship God."
2. The second angel says, "This age is closing, and the ways of this age are judged and doomed to wrath."
3. The third angel says, "Do not receive the mark of the Beast, or suffer the torment of eternal fire and punishment forever."

I find interesting the proclamation of that third angel. The proclamation is important enough to be given special attention. If anyone receives the mark, number, or name of the Beast, they are doomed to eternal punishment. There is no forgiveness. There is no grace. There will be no excuses. There will be no mercy. It doesn't matter if you're male or female. It doesn't matter if you take the mark so that your children can eat. There is only eternal judgment. Do not be deceived.

On the other hand, the hardships that we may endure during this age cannot be compared to the wonders of the ages to come. I believe that is the reason that we are given Revelation 14:12–13, which says, "Here is the patience of the saints: here are they that keep the commandments of God, and the faith of Jesus. And I heard a voice from heaven saying unto me, Write, Blessed are the dead which die in the Lord from henceforth: Yea, saith the Spirit, that they may rest from their labours; and their works do follow them."

Did you see that? Those that are in Christ are laboring. We're laboring and the angels are laboring.

"Here is the patience of the saints; here are those who keep the commandments of God and the faith of Jesus." Why say that? Because this will be a time of great tribulation and persecution. Our patience is tested by standing faithful to the name of Jesus during hunger, persecution, and death. It is our faithfulness that sees us through and brings the blessing. It is our faith and patience that inherits *everlasting* joy. The kingdom of God is an eternal kingdom. It never ceases. It never grows old. God has plans for each and every one of us throughout eternity. That is so real to me that sometimes when I think about eternity, I feel as if I'm going to have and out-of-body experience. But between now and then, there is work to be done.

Jesus has this to say in the book of Luke about the faith and patience of the saints. Luke 21:12, 16–19 says,

> But before all these, they shall lay their hands on you, and persecute you, delivering you up to the synagogues, and into prisons, being brought before kings and rulers for my name's sake … And ye shall be betrayed both by parents, and brethren, and kinsfolks, and friends; and some of you shall they cause to be put to death. And ye shall be hated of all men for my name's sake. But there shall not an hair of your head perish. In your patience possess ye your souls.

Hey! What's your position now? If these things were to take place in your life now, how would you react? Would you be offended at God? Or would God be your source of comfort and strength? What's happening in your life now that makes you want to quit or be depressed? Are you relying on your Savior or running from Him?

Believe it or not, patience isn't a curse from God. It's being steadfast and consistent in your faith and faithfulness in times of stress. We all have to use patience. Nobody is exempt. Not even God. Look how long He took to get Jesus to the earth. Look how long He worked with you until you came to Christ. Look how patient He is with you now. Praise the Lord. God is good!

Listen! Hell is a real place, and many people are going there now. Judgment awaits them. *Eternal punishment* is their final destination. That's a long time. There is no parole. There is no other chance. While we're enjoying eternity, they are without hope of any joy and relief from pain. We're the last chance for these lost souls. God is mustering an army who is willing to go into the last great war. They will be warriors who are willing to give all for Him if necessary so that some may be saved. They will be warriors who may not see the results of their sacrifices until after the war is ended, whose works follow them.

Come on, what do we have to lose? We can only gain. We might as well have something to show for our time in this age. It only happens once and then eternity.

The Rapture

Are you getting the picture of this lesson? This is what it's building up to. To reiterate, this is how the events have developed:

1. Revelation 12 is leading up to the abomination of desolation. Why did the abomination occur?
2. Revelation 13 is what takes place at the time of the abomination of desolation and subsequent events. How will we know the abomination of desolation?
3. Revelation 14 gives an overview from the abomination of desolation to the wrath of God. Where is the rapture in all this, and when does the wrath of God occur?

Many people think that the great tribulation is called the great tribulation because it is a time when the wrath of God is poured out. In fact, the wrath of God is poured out because it is a time of great tribulation. It is a time when sin has reached its fullness and sinners knowingly refuse the gospel. It is a time of chaos and great stress. It is a time when all flesh shall perish if the Son of God does not come. And He does return just in time.

Matthew 24:21–22 says, "For then shall be great tribulation, such as was not since the beginning of the world to this time, no, nor ever shall be. And except those days should be shortened, there should no flesh be saved: but for the elect's sake those days shall be shortened."

Revelation 14:14–16 says,

> And I looked, and behold a white cloud, and upon
> the cloud one sat like unto the Son of man, having
> on his head a golden crown, and in his hand a sharp
> sickle. And another angel came out of the temple,
> crying with a loud voice to him that sat on the
> cloud, Thrust in thy sickle, and reap: for the time
> is come for thee to reap; for the harvest of the earth
> is ripe. And he that sat on the cloud thrust in his
> sickle on the earth; and the earth was reaped.

The Lord of the harvest awaits His precious fruit of the earth.
And when it's time, He reaps. After He reaps, then the wrath of God
is poured out upon those who have rejected salvation.

Revelation 14:17–20 says,

> And another angel came out of the temple which
> is in heaven, he also having a sharp sickle. And
> another angel came out from the altar, which had
> power over fire; and cried with a loud cry to him
> that had the sharp sickle, saying, Thrust in thy
> sharp sickle, and gather the clusters of the vine
> of the earth; for her grapes are fully ripe. And
> the angel thrust in his sickle into the earth, and
> gathered the vine of the earth, and cast it into
> the great winepress of the wrath of God. And the
> winepress was trodden without the city, and blood
> came out of the winepress, even unto the horse
> bridles, by the space of a thousand and six hundred
> furlongs.

We could continue into Revelation 15 and beyond and speak of
the wrath of God, but that is for another time. The purpose of this

chapter, as said before, is to give an outline of events that covers the span between the abomination of desolation to the wrath of God and also covers when the coming of the Lord takes place. We want to know the divine order of the end times so that we're not deceived.

You can see that after the abomination of desolation occurs, there is a time of tribulation before the church is gathered to the Lord, and after our gathering together, the wrath of God is poured out. It's just as Paul wrote the Thessalonians. First Thessalonians 5:9 says, "For God hath not appointed us to wrath, but to obtain salvation by our Lord Jesus Christ."

CHAPTER 6

✦⇒ ⇐✦

A Look at Revelation 15–16

Revelation 15

Revelation 15:1 says, "And I saw another sign in heaven, great and marvellous, seven angels having the seven last plagues; for in them is filled up the wrath of God." The wrath of God is complete in these seven last plagues, but we are not destined for the wrath of God as we can see in 1 Thessalonians 5:9, which says, "For God hath not appointed us to wrath, but to obtain salvation by our Lord Jesus Christ."

Revelation 15:2–4 says,

> For *Your judgments have been manifested.* And I saw as it were a sea of glass mingled with fire: *and them that had gotten the victory over the beast, and over his image, and over his mark, and over the number of his name*, stand on the sea of glass, having the harps of God. And they sing the song of Moses the servant of God, and the song of the Lamb, saying, Great and marvellous are thy works, Lord God Almighty; just and true are thy ways, thou King of saints. Who shall not fear thee, O Lord, and glorify thy name? for thou only art holy: for all nations shall come and worship before thee; *for thy judgments are made manifest.* (emphasis mine)

God did not appoint us to wrath, and we can see in Revelation 15:2–4 that those who do not bow to the Beast are not on the earth when the bowls of wrath are poured out. We can see that they were on the earth at the time of the abomination of desolation and the mark of the Beast because they have "the victory over the beast." Notice that God's "judgments have been manifested." This tells me that people have had ample opportunity to repent prior to the manifestation of the Lord and the time when the bowls of the wrath of God are poured out. Take the time to read the first twelve chapters of Exodus. You'll see that Israel was subject to the first three plagues. During the fourth plague, the Bible says, "And I will sever in that day the land of Goshen, in which my people dwell" (Exodus 8:22).

There is certainly scriptural precedence for the saints to see tribulation. But we also see that the worst times were reserved for the ungodly and unrepentant.

Revelation 15:5–8 says,

> And after that I looked, and, behold, the temple of the tabernacle of the testimony in heaven was opened: And the seven angels came out of the temple, having the seven plagues, clothed in pure and white linen, and having their breasts girded with golden girdles. And one of the four beasts gave unto the seven angels seven golden vials full of the wrath of God, who liveth for ever and ever. And the temple was filled with smoke from the glory of God, and from his power; and no man was able to enter into the temple, till the seven plagues of the seven angels were fulfilled.

Here it specifically states that God is pouring out His wrath. In Revelation 16, we're going to find out what that wrath consists of. But notice that when God was ready to inflict the earth with His wrath, no one was able to enter the temple till the seven plagues of the seven angels were completed. God does not want to pour out His indignation; however, when He does, it's something that's personal, and he doesn't want others to be a part of it.

Revelation 16

Revelation 16:1 says, "And I heard a great voice out of the temple saying to the seven angels, Go your ways, and pour out the vials of the wrath of God upon the earth."

We're going to find out now what the wrath of God will be.

Bowls of Wrath

I've chosen an outline presentation for the bowls of wrath. I believe it makes it easier on the reader to follow and grasp the severity each plague.

1. Revelation 16:1
   a. It's poured out on the earth.
   b. It's a foul and loathsome sore upon those who have the mark of the Beast and those who worship his image.
2. Revelation 16:3
   a. It's poured out on the sea.
   b. The sea becomes blood, and every creature in the sea dies.
3. Revelation 16:4–7
   a. It's poured out on the rivers and springs.
   b. They become as blood.
4. Revelation 16:8–9
   a. It's poured out on the sun.
   b. People are scorched with great heat.
5. Revelation 16:10–11
   a. It's poured out on the throne of the Beast.

      b.   The Beast's kingdom is full of darkness.

      c.   Those in the Beast's kingdom are full of pain and sores.

  6.   Revelation 16:12–16

      a.   It's poured out into the Euphrates River.

      b.   The Euphrates is dried up.

  7.   Revelation 16:17-21

      a.   It's poured out into the air.

      b.   There are noises, thundering, and lightning.

      c.   There is a great earthquake. The great city divides into three parts, and the cities of all the nations fall. Every island disappears, and all the mountains fall.

      d.   Seventy-five-pound balls of hail descend to the earth.

      e.   Babylon is remembered.

As you read Revelation 16, take note that the inhabitants of the earth don't repent of their sins. They know God has power over the plagues that are happening, yet they refuse to repent. It seems incredible, but it's true. These people have utterly refused to have God in their thinking. They are totally given over to the Antichrist. We see Paul make mention of this in his letters. Look again at 2 Thessalonians 2:9–10, which says, "Even him, whose coming is after the working of Satan with all power and signs and lying wonders, And with all deceivableness of unrighteousness in them that perish; *because they received not the love of the truth*, that they might be saved" (emphasis mine).

They don't want to know the truth. They have made up their minds that the God of heaven is less than men. They worship the Antichrist. Even with all the pain and tragedies that have taken place and even with the two mighty witnesses we read of in Revelation 11, they believe *the lie*—that the lawless one is God. They see the lying power, signs, and wonders and choose to believe what the Beast says rather than the witness of the gospel and the demonstration of the power of God. Lying signs are signs that point you in the wrong direction.

Second Thessalonians 2:11–12 says, "And for this cause God shall send them strong delusion, that they should believe a lie: That they all might be damned who believed not the truth, but had pleasure in unrighteousness." Revelation 16:12–14 says,

> And the sixth angel poured out his vial upon the great river Euphrates; and the water thereof was dried up, that the way of the kings of the east might be prepared. And I saw three unclean spirits like frogs come out of the mouth of the dragon, and out of the mouth of the beast, and out of the mouth of the false prophet. *For they are the spirits of devils, working miracles*, which go forth unto the kings of the earth and of the whole world, to gather them to the battle of that great day of God Almighty. (emphasis mine)

The *strong delusion* that God sends them is the allowance of these spirits of demons, performing signs to be released into the earth through the devil, the Antichrist, and the false prophet. Amazingly, even when Jesus appears, the signs of the Antichrist persuade the rulers of the earth that they have a chance to win against God. Or perhaps they know they have nothing to lose and figure they must try. Satan will perform many signs and wonders during the Antichrist's reign. He'll use anyone who will yield to him.

Matthew 24:24 says, "For there shall arise false Christs, and false prophets, and shall shew great signs and wonders; insomuch that, if it were possible, they shall deceive the very elect."

We can see an example of the attitude during the Beast's reign by reading about Pharaoh and Moses. Pharaoh was pompous, arrogant, and prideful until the night that the Lord came and delivered his people. Perhaps this will help us to understand what Jesus said in Revelation 16:15, "Behold, I come as a thief. Blessed is he that watcheth, and keepeth his garments, lest he walk naked, and they see his shame."

What if someone isn't watching or isn't keeping his garments? They will be deceived. God will reveal His plan to those who are preparing and heeding His word, but He also knows how to hide what He's doing from those who reject His call.

Pharaoh and Egypt saw the power of God work many times. Miracles were done then that we have never seen since. Yet believing a lie can be so strong, and pride can be so powerful that a man will throw his life away instead of repenting. Satan fell because of these very reasons, and he walked in the very presence of God. In Egypt, we see those who refused to give credit to God and His prophet in the case of the plague of hail. Exodus 9:20–21, 25 says, "He that feared the word of the Lord among the servants of Pharaoh made his servants and his cattle flee into the houses: And he that regarded not the word of the Lord left his servants and his cattle in the field … And the hail smote throughout all the land of Egypt all that was in the field, both man and beast."

You would think that by this time, the seventh plague, a sensible man wouldn't have made his people stay in the field and perish. But their loyalty to their *god* caused them to believe a lie. Jesus said to watch (Revelation 16:15; Mark 13:33-37). How do we do this? We do this by watching through the truth of the word of God. Jesus said that we should not be deceived and that the very elect will be affected if we don't watch. In other words, stay on the alert.

First Peter 5:8–9 says, "Be sober, be vigilant; because your adversary the devil, as a roaring lion, walketh about, seeking whom he may devour: Whom resist stedfast in the faith." James 1:21–22 says, "Wherefore lay apart all filthiness and superfluity of naughtiness, and receive with meekness the engrafted word, which is able to save your souls. But be ye doers of the word, and not hearers only, deceiving your own selves."

Keepeth his garments, (Revelation 16:15) is the same as saying *lay aside all filthiness and overflow of wickedness.* It's the same warning that Jesus gave in Matthew 24:48–50, which says, "But and if that evil servant shall say in his heart, My lord delayeth his coming; And shall begin to smite his fellowservants, and to eat and drink with the drunken; The lord of that servant shall come in a day when he looketh not for him, and in an hour that he is not aware of."

As a wise man once said, "If you act like the devil, look like the devil, and talk like the devil, you is the devil." And you'll get the devil's reward. God knows that you're not perfect, and He's not looking to find fault with you. Forgiveness is available to those who have acted like the devil. God isn't a fool either. He knows your heart and motives. Be quick to repent and forgive and be ready for the Lord's return.

Try to take a bird's-eye view of what will happen on the earth when the wrath of God is poured out. Men are scorched with great heat. It would appear that whatever protection our atmosphere provides from the sun will be greatly diminished. Water is scarce because its sources have been turned into blood. The Euphrates is dried up. Food is scarce because of the great heat and draughts. Darkness and pain are prevalent. Seventy-five-pound hails are crashing to the earth. And an earthquake occurs that flattens mountains and drowns islands. Isaiah 13:9–12 states,

Behold, *the day of the Lord cometh,cruel both with wrath and fierce anger,* to lay the land desolate: and he shall destroy the sinners thereof out of it. For the stars of heaven and the constellations thereof shall not give their light: the sun shall be darkened in his going forth, and the moon shall not cause her light to shine. And I will punish the world for their evil, and the wicked for their iniquity; and I will cause the arrogancy of the proud to cease, and will lay low the haughtiness of the terrible. I will make a man more precious than fine gold; even a man than the golden wedge of Ophir. Therefore I will shake the heavens, and the earth shall remove out of her place, *in the wrath of the Lord of hosts, and in the day of his fierce anger.* (emphasis mine)

By the time the millennial reign starts, the mortal men left on the earth will be as rare as gold.

That's just what is happening in the natural. Demonic powers

CHAPTER 7

⤝⟹ ⟸⤞

A Look at Revelation 17–18

Revelation 17: Babylon Revealed

Revelation 17:1–2 says, "And there came one of the seven angels which had the seven vials, and talked with me, saying unto me, Come hither; I will shew unto thee the judgment of the great whore that sitteth upon many waters: With whom the kings of the earth have committed fornication, and the inhabitants of the earth have been made drunk with the wine of her fornication."

According to the angel, what God is about to reveal to us is the judgment of the harlot who has so much sway over the peoples of the earth. Why do you suppose she is called a *great harlot*? It's because she's a seductress that lures people away from God. She entices people to have an affair with the things of this world and not worship the living God, the Creator of all things. People are drunk with the desire of the things of this life—entertainment, sex, political power, social influence, money, fame, and anything else that draws a person away from serving the God of creation and His Son, Jesus, the Messiah.

How the Antichrist Entices

Revelation 17:3 says, "So he carried me away in the spirit into the wilderness: and I saw a woman sit upon a scarlet coloured beast, full of names of blasphemy, having seven heads and ten horns."

I want you to notice first the beast. It has *seven heads and ten horns*. In Revelation 13:1, you'll see this is the same beast. Revelation 13:1 says, "And I stood upon the sand of the sea, and saw a beast rise up out of the sea, *having seven heads and ten horns*, and upon his horns ten crowns, and upon his heads the name of blasphemy" (emphasis mine).

This beast is the Antichrist. Take note that the Beast also looks much like his father, the devil, the fiery red dragon of Revelation 12. The Antichrist uses the woman to manipulate and control the world through the lust of the flesh and the deceitfulness of riches. He promises liberty and prosperity through beautiful promises and lying signs and wonders, but the end result for his followers is only eternal darkness and fire.

The woman seduces her victims to sin. Sin causes prosperity to become poverty, and death is the end result. In other words, sin causes whatever it seduces to become a wilderness. James brings this out in his letter.

James 1:14–16 says, "But every man is tempted, when he is drawn away of his own lust, and enticed. Then when lust hath conceived, it bringeth forth sin: and sin, when it is finished, bringeth forth death. Do not err, my beloved brethren."

Death is the end result of sin. Sin doesn't start off looking like death. If you were to have a lion cub as a pet, at first it would be a cuddly pet. You may not recognize it at first, but it still has wild animal instincts. When that cub reaches maturity, it has the power to destroy you. Sin is the same way. And in the end, that demon you allowed in your life will kill you with the very thing that you enjoyed at the beginning. Sin becomes your dungeon until your death. Paul makes this clear in his letter to the Romans. Romans

6:16 says, "Know ye not, that to whom ye yield yourselves servants to obey, his servants ye are to whom ye obey; whether of sin unto death, or of obedience unto righteousness?"

The death of prosperity and health equals an empty wilderness that is uninhabitable. Satan destroys individuals, families, and nations through the great harlot. The beast that the harlot rides is full of the names of blasphemy. He hates God and righteousness. His companion, the harlot, looks beautiful but brings with her all unrighteousness, ungodliness, and death.

The wilderness is wherever Hades is in manifestation. It's whatever the Devil controls. Spiritually, the earth is a wilderness infested with demonic spirits. Isaiah reveals Satan's destructive nature. Isaiah 14:16–17 says, "They that see thee shall narrowly look upon thee, and consider thee, saying, Is this the man that made the earth to tremble, that did shake kingdoms; *That made the world as a wilderness*, and destroyed the cities thereof; that opened not the house of his prisoners?" (emphasis mine).

Jesus said, "The thief cometh not, but for to steal, and to kill, and to destroy: I am come that they might have life, and that they might have it more abundantly" (John 10:10). Anything that kills, steals, and destroys causes prosperity to become a wilderness. Satan is the maker of wildernesses.

Let's look at some of the pleasures of sin that kill, steal, and destroy.

The Abominations of Babylon

Revelation 17:4–6 says,

> And the woman was arrayed in purple and scarlet colour, and decked with gold and precious stones and pearls, having a golden cup in her hand full of abominations and filthiness of her fornication: And upon her forehead was a name written, Mystery,

> Babylon the Great, the Mother of harlots and abominations of the earth. And I saw the woman drunken with the blood of the saints, and with the blood of the martyrs of Jesus: and when I saw her, I wondered with great admiration.

The great harlot is very beautiful on the outside, but on the inside she is very evil. The sin that she offers always comes wrapped in something beautiful (a golden cup). But the sins that are in that beautiful golden cup are detestable things of a filthy life. Through her seductions, she causes those who are enticed to persecute and murder followers of the holy God and His Son, Jesus.

What kinds of things are in that golden cup?

Deuteronomy 18:9–12 says,

> When thou art come into the land which the Lord thy God giveth thee, thou shalt not learn to do after the *abominations* of those nations. There shall not be found among you any one that maketh his son or his daughter to pass through the fire, or that useth divination, or an observer of times, or an enchanter, or a witch, Or a charmer, or a consulter with familiar spirits, or a wizard, or a necromancer. For all that do these things are an *abomination* unto the Lord: and because of these *abominations* the Lord thy God doth drive them out from before thee. (emphasis mine)

Deuteronomy 27:15; 7:25 then says, "Cursed be the man that maketh any graven or molten image, an *abomination* unto the Lord … The graven images of their gods shall ye burn with fire: thou shalt not desire the silver or gold that is on them, nor take it unto thee, lest thou be snared therein: for it is an *abomination* to the Lord thy God" (emphasis mine).

So far we're beginning to see quite a list of things that the Lord declares are in the harlot's cup of abominations. Shall I review them? There's (1) child sacrifice. In our modern times, we would be horrified with the burning of our children. But I'm sure that in the eyes of God, aborting babies the way we do falls into this category. There's also (2) witchcraft. God doesn't distinguish between *black* or *white* witchcraft. It's all from the devil. It's just packaged differently to appeal to the lust of the flesh and the vanity of different people's desires. Then there's (3) soothsaying (fortune-telling), (4) interpreting omens, (5) sorcery, (6) conjuring spells, (7) acting as a medium, (8) spiritism, (9) serving as one who calls up the dead, and (10) idolatry.

Leviticus 18:21–25 says,

> And thou shalt not let any of thy seed pass through the fire to Molech, neither shalt thou profane the name of thy God: I am the Lord. Thou shalt not lie with mankind, as with womankind: it is *abomination*. Neither shalt thou lie with any beast to defile thyself therewith: neither shall any woman stand before a beast to lie down thereto: it is confusion. Defile not ye yourselves in any of these things: for in all these the nations are defiled which I cast out before you: And the land is defiled: therefore I do visit the iniquity thereof upon it, and the land itself vomiteth out her inhabitants. (emphasis mine)

Other abominable practices are human sacrifices, homosexuality, and bestiality. Because of these things, the nations are punished. In fact, "the land vomiteth out her inhabitants." The earth itself rebels against sin.

Romans 8:18–22 says,

> For I reckon that the sufferings of this present time are not worthy to be compared with the glory which

shall be revealed in us. For the earnest expectation of the creature waiteth for the manifestation of the sons of God. For the creature was made subject to vanity, not willingly, but by reason of him who hath subjected the same in hope, Because the creature itself also shall be delivered from the bondage of corruption into the glorious liberty of the children of God.

The earth is in bondage to the corruption of man's sins until the time when Jesus appears and restores righteousness. Satan will be locked up, and there will be no demonic activity during the millennial reign of Christ. But until then, the earth is subject to destruction that sin brings. An interesting scripture in Isaiah bears witness with this. Isaiah 24:19–20 says, "The earth is utterly broken down, the earth is clean dissolved, the earth is moved exceedingly. The earth shall reel to and fro like a drunkard, and shall be removed like a cottage; and the transgression thereof shall be heavy upon it; and it shall fall, and not rise again."

The cause of the flood of Noah was sin. The cause of the tribulation and the wrath of God is sin. The earth can only stand so much pressure before it begins to destruct. God judges sin in order to save His people and the earth from being utterly destroyed. Matthew 24:22 says, "And except those days should be shortened, there should no flesh be saved: but for the elect's sake those days shall be shortened." The earth will be utterly destroyed because of the destructive, sinful nature of man if Jesus doesn't return.

Wearing the clothing of the opposite's sex is an abomination. Deuteronomy 22:5 say, "The woman shall not wear that which pertaineth unto a man, neither shall a man put on a woman's garment: for all that do so are *abomination* unto the Lord thy God" (emphasis mine)

Deuteronomy 25:13–16 declares that false weights and measures are an abomination. And of course, the list in Proverbs is quite clear. Proverbs 6:16–19 says, "These six things doth the Lord hate: yea, seven are an *abomination* unto him: A proud look, a lying tongue, and hands that shed innocent blood, An heart that deviseth wicked imaginations, feet that be swift in running to mischief, A false witness that speaketh lies, and he that soweth discord among brethren" (emphasis mine).

All of these abominations are in the cup of the great harlot. With these detestable things, she seduces the inhabitants of the earth and causes destruction and judgment to come on the earth. And through the great harlot, Satan manipulates and seduces the multitudes to follow him. Satan's final strategy is using the son of perdition, the Antichrist.

Daniel 8:23–25 (NKJV) says,

> And in the latter time of their kingdom, *when the transgressors have reached their fullness*, a king shall arise, having fierce features, who understands sinister schemes. His power shall be mighty, but not by his own power; he shall prosper and thrive; he shall destroy the mighty, and also the holy people. Through his cunning *he shall cause deceit to prosper* under his rule; and he shall exalt himself in his heart. He shall destroy many in their prosperity. He shall even rise against the Prince of princes; but he shall be broken without human means. (emphasis mine)

"When the transgressors have reached their fullness … he shall cause deceit to prosper." As people drink their fill of the cup of abominations, then deceit shall prosper. In this passage in Daniel, the harlot is riding the Antichrist, deceiving the whole earth, and persecuting the people of God.

The Beginning of Babylon

Revelation 18:21 says, "And a mighty angel took up a stone like a great millstone, and cast it into the sea, saying, Thus with violence shall that great city Babylon be thrown down, and shall be found no more at all."

Here, Babylon is referred to as a city. There's no contradiction. Whether described as a harlot or a city, the description fits. Babylon is the world's system that is motivated by the lust of the flesh and led by the prince of the power of the air, Satan. I'll give you a little background of Babylon, and perhaps you'll see something new. Let's read something that Josephus wrote. Josephus (AD 37–100) was a Jewish historian. His extra-biblical writings of the first century are compiled in *The Works of Josephus*. Though his works aren't scripture, they can be enlightening on the thoughts and customs of the Jewish people in the first century AD. The following quotes are taken from chapter 4 of Josephus's work *Antiquities of the Jews* chapter IV.

> Now it was Nimrod who excited them to such an affront and contempt of God. He was grandson of Ham, the son of Noah, - a bold man, and of great strength of hand. He persuaded them not to ascribe it to God, as if it was through his means they were happy, but to believe that it was their own courage which procured that happiness. He also gradually changed the government into tyranny, - seeing no other way of turning men from the fear of God, but to bring them into a constant dependence upon his power. He also said he would be avenged on God, if He should have a mind to drown the world again; for that he would build a tower too high for the waters to be able to reach! And that he would avenge himself on God for destroying their forefathers.

> Now the multitude were very ready to follow
> the determination of Nimrod, and to esteem it a
> cowardice to submit to God; and they built a tower.

Nimrod was the great-grandson of Noah, and he built many cities, one of which was Babel. Babel is the Hebrew name and is also known as Babylon. Genesis 10:8, 10 says, "And Cush begat Nimrod: he began to be a mighty one in the earth ... And the beginning of his kingdom was Babel."

Babylon seems to be the chief city of his empire, and this is where he purposed to build the Tower of Babel. This city was the political, economic, and religious center of his empire. Nimrod wanted to turn men from God to himself, but Noah's flood was still in the forefront of people's minds. Through sinister schemes, Nimrod enticed the multitudes to his will. He came to great power, and through tyranny, he caused the multitude to turn from God and bring them to a dependence upon his power. He came to the place where he degraded God to a human or perhaps subhuman level and exalted himself to the place of being God. Nimrod set himself up as God, building a temple (the tower) for himself to show himself and others that he was greater than God. He declared vengeance on God because God had destroyed the peoples' forefathers by Noah's flood. It's not unlike the modern humanist/atheist retort of God being unsympathetic and cruel to the animals by destroying them in Noah's flood. It's a method of manipulation and insolence. The tower is a sign of defiance toward God. It is an image that declares rebellion against God and submission to Nimrod's authority. The tower was a declaration that God's judgment can't reach us anymore. It was the *abomination of desolation* for that time. The multitude followed Nimrod. They became so deceived they considered it cowardice to submit to God. Essentially, the idea behind the tower was a place of protection against another flood, showing the might of Nimrod's power. God destroyed the tower and the will of the people of that time by confusing the languages of the multitudes.

Whether or not Josephus's description is correct, this is how the Jewish people would have understood Babylon. If Babylon was mentioned in conversation or in a sermon, these thoughts would be the underpinning of their thinking. When John wrote of Babylon in the book of Revelation, he would have had these thoughts. By the description and attitude the Bible takes of Babylon, I'd say Josephus's description is valid enough to take seriously. The point is this is a good example of the premillennial Antichrist world.

Striking Similarities between Josephus's Writings and the Biblical Description of the Antichrist

First, they both desire a kingdom free from the influence of God. Josephus stated, "Now it was Nimrod who excited them to such an affront and contempt of God ... and they built a tower." The new testament describes the antichrist in like manner. Second Thessalonians 2:3–4 says, "Let no man deceive you by any means: for that day shall not come, except there come a falling away first, and that man of sin be revealed, the son of perdition; Who opposeth and exalteth himself above all that is called God, or that is worshipped; so that he as God sitteth in the temple of God, shewing himself that he is God." And Revelation 13:8 says, "And all that dwell upon the earth shall worship him."

Second, they're both bold with a charismatic appeal. Josephus describes Nimrod as "a bold man, and of great strength of hand." And Revelation 13:4, 8 elucidates the Beast saying, "And they worshipped the dragon which gave power unto the beast: and they worshipped the beast, saying, Who is like unto the beast? who is able to make war with him? ... And all that dwell upon the earth shall worship him."

Third, Nimrod and the Antichrist persuaded his followers not to give credit to God for the good things in their lives. Josephus states, "He persuaded them not to ascribe it to God, as if it was through his means they were happy, but to believe that it was their own courage which procured that happiness." Revelation 13:16–17 says of the lawless one, "And he causeth all, both small and great, rich and poor, free and bond, to receive a mark in their right hand, or in their foreheads: And that no man might buy or sell, save he that had the mark, or the name of the beast, or the number of his name."

Fourth, they're both tyrants. Josephus states, "He also gradually changed the government into tyranny, - seeing no other way of turning men from the fear of God, but to bring them into a constant dependence upon his power." And Revelation 13:5–7 says, "And there was given unto him a mouth speaking great things and blasphemies ... And he opened his mouth in blasphemy against God, to blaspheme his name, and his tabernacle, and them that dwell in heaven. And it was given unto him to make war with the saints, and to overcome them: and power was given him over all kindreds, and tongues, and nations." So too, Daniel 7:23–25 says,

> Thus he said, The fourth beast shall be the fourth kingdom upon earth, which shall be diverse from all kingdoms, and shall devour the whole earth, and shall tread it down, and break it in pieces. And the ten horns out of this kingdom are ten kings that shall arise: and another shall rise after them; and he shall be diverse from the first, and he shall subdue three kings. And he shall speak great words against the most High, and shall wear out the saints of the most High, and think to change times and laws: and they shall be given into his hand until a time and times and the dividing of time

Fifth, the majority of the people are willing to follow the Antichrist or Nimrod. Josephus states, "Now the multitude were very ready to follow the determination of Nimrod, and to esteem it a cowardice to submit to God." Revelation 13:8 says, "And all that dwell upon the earth shall worship him, whose names are not written in the book of life of the Lamb slain from the foundation of the world."

I think we can see why the whore is named Babylon and why she rides the Beast. Satan's social, economic, and political system is a seductress that entices people into rebellion against God.

Revelation 18: Babylon Is Fallen

Revelation 18:1–2 says, "And after these things I saw another angel come down from heaven, having great power; and the earth was lightened with his glory. And he cried mightily with a strong voice, saying, Babylon the great is fallen, is fallen, and is become the habitation of devils, and the hold of every foul spirit, and a cage of every unclean and hateful bird."

Jesus said that his people are the salt of the earth and the light of the world. When His people are taken out of the earth, there will be no one left in the earth with the blessing of God. The curse of sin will be in full manifestation. The reason that the systems of the world haven't fallen already is because God's blessing is on his people.

Genesis 12:1–3 says, "Now the Lord had said unto Abram, Get thee out of thy country, and from thy kindred, and from thy father's house, unto a land that I will shew thee: And I will make of thee a great nation, *and I will bless thee, and make thy name great; and thou shalt be a blessing*: And I will bless them that bless thee, and curse him that curseth thee: *and in thee shall all families of the earth be blessed*" (emphasis mine).

Galatians 3:13–14, 29 says, "Christ hath redeemed us from the curse of the law, being made a curse for us: for it is written, Cursed is every one that hangeth on a tree: *That the blessing of Abraham might come on the Gentiles through Jesus Christ*; that we might receive the promise of the Spirit through faith … *And if ye be Christ's, then are ye Abraham's seed, and heirs according to the promise*" (emphasis mine).

The world is blessed when we walk in the blessing of God. God reaches the world through us. When Jesus takes his own out of the earth, Babylon's ruin is imminent. The motivations and operations of the world system—the abominations, the greed, the murders, the lies and deceits, slavery, and selfishness—are judged and condemned. The fruit of its sowing is the wine it must partake of. It will disappear forever.

Revelation 18:15–17, 19 says,

> The merchants of these things, which were made rich by her, shall stand afar off for the fear of her torment, weeping and wailing, And saying, Alas, alas, that great city, that was clothed in fine linen, and purple, and scarlet, and decked with gold, and precious stones, and pearls! For in one hour so great riches is come to nought ... And they cast dust on their heads, and cried, weeping and wailing, saying, Alas, alas, that great city, wherein were made rich all that had ships in the sea by reason of her costliness! for in one hour is she made desolate.

Not in one place do we read of those who wept over Babylon that they shed one tear for any human being. Their hearts are revealed. They love things and use people. With God, one loves people and uses things.

Revelation 18:22–24 says,

> And the voice of harpers, and musicians, and of pipers, and trumpeters, shall be heard no more at all in thee; and no craftsman, of whatsoever craft he be, shall be found any more in thee; and the sound of a millstone shall be heard no more at all in thee; And the light of a candle shall shine no more at all in thee; and the voice of the bridegroom and

> of the bride shall be heard no more at all in thee: for
> thy merchants were the great men of the earth; for
> by thy sorceries were all nations deceived. And in
> her was found the blood of prophets, and of saints,
> and of all that were slain upon the earth.

Going forward from the destruction of Babylon, the nations will live according to rules of the kingdom of heaven. Jesus will reign. "And he shall rule them with a rod of iron; as the vessels of a potter shall they be broken to shivers" (Revelation 2:27). In other words, the sins and system of Babylon shall no longer be tolerated.

Revelation 18:4 says, "And I heard another voice from heaven, saying, Come out of her, my people, that ye be not partakers of her sins, and that ye receive not of her plagues." God wouldn't command us to come out if we didn't the choice to stay. It also means that God has a different way for us to live. We are to live by faith that God will supply all of our needs according to his riches in glory by Christ Jesus (Philippians 4:19). We are not to put our faith in the world's system—politicians, companies, unions, fraternities, and the like. This is certainly not to say that we are to do without government, laws, jobs, or system of commerce and such. But we are to put our faith in God, not in the things that are in the world. As I said before, the mark of the Beast is a commitment to him as provider. Faith in Jesus is a commitment to God as provider. If you're worried about gasoline prices increasing, what is your faith in? If you're voting based on what you can get instead of who is godly, who is your faith in? As the five virgins in Matthew 25 were prepared for the coming of the bridegroom, before Jesus returns and takes His own, His own will have made herself known in whom she trusts.

CHAPTER 8

✦⟫⟨✦

The Beast and then the Horn

Daniel 9:26–27; 7:7–8

Daniel 9:26–27 (NKJV) says,

> And after the sixty-two weeks Messiah shall be
> cut off, but not for Himself; and the *people of the
> prince who is to come* shall destroy the city and the
> sanctuary. The end of it shall be with a flood, and
> till the end of the war desolations are determined.
> *Then he* shall confirm a covenant with many for
> one week; but in the middle of the week he shall
> bring an end to sacrifice and offering. And on the
> wing of abominations shall be one who makes
> desolate, even until the consummation, which
> is determined, is poured out on the desolate.
> (emphasis mine)

We know that after Jesus went to the cross, Jerusalem fell.
(Oftentimes prophecy may have a dual meaning.) But the primary
point of this passage isn't in reference to the Romans' conquest of
Jerusalem. I say this because verse 27 says *then*. After the fall of
Jerusalem, *"then he* shall confirm a covenant with many for one

week; but in the middle of the week *he shall bring an end to sacrifice and offering.*"

Now hang in there! I'll back this up and show you why I say this. But let me bring out a few points on this scripture.

The "people of the prince who is to come" shall destroy the city and the sanctuary. Initially, this people will do the destroying, and *then* the prince shall come. These people will cause great war and destruction: Verse 26 says, "And till the end of the war desolations are determined."

Desolation means ruin, wasteland, and rendered unfit for habitation or use. The army that brings about this war will care little of anything but conquering. But what happens at the end of the war?

Verse 27 says, "Then he shall confirm a covenant with many for one week." A covenant that brings peace from the destruction will be brought about by the Antichrist. Sacrifice and offering will be instituted, but in the middle of the agreement, he brings an end to it. This Antichrist makes a covenant with *many*. Many nations and powerful people will partake of his plan and fall into the trap of the devil. Though this man brings peace, the peace will turn into bloodshed, and the prosperity into famine.

Verse 27 continues, "Then he shall confirm a covenant with many for one week; but in the middle of the week he shall bring an end to sacrifice and offering."

He breaks the covenant of peace in the middle of the contract of peace. Think of how easy and how quickly all this can take place. With the Middle East in a chaotic mess, the EU running dry economically and beginning to splinter into nationalist interests, the United States and China facing economic collapse, and a whole world literally decaying economically, socially, and environmentally, it would take very little to cause a great war. The world would gladly follow anyone who could bring peace. Even the Muslims would follow this person if they believed he was their Mahdi. This is the very scenario that will happen. And in the middle of a time of peace and prosperity, when the world thinks it is safe, sudden destruction shall come on them.

First Thessalonians 5:3 says, "For when they shall say, Peace and safety; then sudden destruction cometh upon them, as travail upon a woman with child; and they shall not escape." Daniel 9:27 says, "And for the overspreading of abominations he shall make it desolate."

The scripture is reminiscent of the warning that Jesus gave. Matthew 24:15, 21 says, "When ye therefore shall see the abomination of desolation, spoken of by Daniel the prophet, stand in the holy place ... For then shall be great tribulation, such as was not since the beginning of the world to this time, no, nor ever shall be."

On the wing of the abomination of desolation shall be one who causes great desolate tribulation. As the appellation denotes, an abominable thing will give cause for despair, anguish, and misery. In other words, the appearance of the abomination of desolation (when the Antichrist declares his supremacy) causes the great tribulation. Abominate means to detest and abhor. Therefore, he causes ruin by things that are detestable and abhorrent.

Now let's look at Daniel 7.

Daniel 7

As we study the beasts that rise to power, I want to make clear that I don't claim to have all the answers. What I'm sharing with you are the revelations that stand out to me. I hope that they're a help for you.

Stirring of the Great Sea

Daniel 7:1–2 (NKJV) says, "In the first year of Belshazzar King of Babylon, Daniel had a dream and visions of his head while on his bed. Then he wrote down the dream, telling the main facts. Daniel spoke, saying, 'I saw in my vision by night, and behold, the four winds of heaven were stirring up the Great Sea.'"

What is the Great Sea, and what does this describe?

Revelation 17:1, 15 says, "And there came one of the seven angels which had the seven vials, and talked with me, saying unto me, Come hither; I will shew unto thee the judgment of the great whore that sitteth upon many waters. And he saith unto me, The waters which thou sawest, where the whore sitteth, are peoples, and multitudes, and nations, and tongues." Revelation 13:1, 8 says, "And I stood upon the sand of the sea, and saw a beast rise up out of the sea ... And all that dwell upon the earth shall worship him, whose names are not written in the book of life of the Lamb slain from the foundation of the world."

The *Great Sea* describes the sea of the people of the earth—*the people, multitudes, nations, and tongues.*

What are the *four winds of heaven*? We know that they're "stirring up the Great Sea." They're causing trouble, acting tumultuous. Revelation 12:9 says, "And the great dragon was cast out, that old serpent, called the Devil, and Satan, which deceiveth the whole world: he was cast out into the earth, and his angels were cast out with him." First Peter 5:8 says, "Be sober, be vigilant; because your adversary the devil, as a roaring lion, walketh about, seeking whom he may devour."

We see from this that the devil is the great deceiver looking for someone to devour, and when he rebelled, he had followers that fell from grace with him. Ephesians 6:12 says, "For we wrestle not against flesh and blood, but against principalities, against powers, against the rulers of the darkness of this world, against spiritual wickedness in high places."

Principalities, powers, rulers of the darkness, and the spiritual wickedness in high places—these are the beings who followed Satan in the great rebellion. These are the *four winds of heaven* that are stirring up the *Great Sea*.

"Stirring up the Great Sea" means they are creating a great storm. It means the peoples of the earth are agitated, unsettled, frustrated, and becoming violent. Things are becoming chaotic and dangerous. Fear is taking over. It's the spiritual equivalent to Noah's flood.

The Four Great Beasts

Daniel 7:3 says, "And four great beasts came up from the sea, diverse one from another."

Out of this stirring come four great beasts. For clarity, keep in mind that each beast represents a belief system. That is how Satan manipulates people. He deceives them into believing a lie. Second Thessalonians 2:9–12 (NKJV) says, "The coming of the lawless one is according to the working of Satan, with all power, signs, and lying wonders, and with all unrighteous deception among those who perish, because they did not receive the love of the truth, that they might be saved. And for this reason God will send them strong delusion, that they should believe the lie, that they all may be condemned who did not believe the truth but had pleasure in unrighteousness."

The four great beasts are four prominent belief systems that have captured the world and have set the world against Christ and his church. We also need to be aware that these beasts are alive at the same time. Daniel 7:12 says, "As concerning the rest of the beasts, they had their dominion taken away: yet their lives were prolonged for a season and time." When we put this scripture passage in context, we find that after the fourth beast is destroyed, the other beasts have *their dominion taken away.* (These rudimentary beliefs will be the resurrected Gog and Magog of Revelation 20:7.) This makes it clear that all four beasts are on the earth at the same time. Furthermore, the four winds of heaven are stirring up the Great Sea, bringing about the four beasts from the same great storm.

The First Beast

Daniel 7:4 says, "The first was like a lion, and had eagle's wings: I beheld till the wings thereof were plucked, and it was lifted up from the earth, and made stand upon the feet as a man, and a man's heart was given to it."

The first beast is humanism. "A man's heart was given to it" speaks to me as humanism. Humanism is man declaring himself as the only savior of mankind and that there is no God. Humanism has been around for centuries but never rose to popularity until Charles Darwin wrote *The Origin of Species*. From there, humanism exploded. The supposed viable proof of evolution gave room for the antireligious to believe in something other than God.

Humanism is a religion. (In fact, all belief systems are religions.) With the increase of scientific research leading to intelligent design/creation origin, *The Origin of Species* and evolution theory doesn't hold up. So why do the intelligentsia cling to the theory of evolution? Because for them it's not a theory. A theory is a belief that one is willing to change when the facts point elsewhere. A belief system is different. Giving up a way of believing in the face of opposition is nigh impossible without someone interceding in prayer for the individual. Evolution isn't a theory for most. It's a religion. Humanism and evolution are two sides to one coin. People connect their whole lives, their hopes, and their ideas of death to belief systems that state there is no God. Because they acknowledge no God, their thoughts are open to every way of life that runs contrary to God. For them it's only logical to live for immediate pleasures and an unrestrained lifestyle. It also opens them up more readily for the second beast to devour them.

The Second Beast

Daniel 7:5 says, "And behold another beast, a second, like to a bear, and it raised up itself on one side, and it had three ribs in the mouth of it between the teeth of it: and they said thus unto it, Arise, devour much flesh."

The three ribs had an agenda. They commanded the bear, "Arise, devour much flesh." Their agenda was to conquer, to spread their beliefs to the multitude, and to consume the masses.

The second beast is represented by the three ribs, specifically (1) Marxism, (2) Socialism, and (3) Communism. They have the same agenda and basic tenets of faith. They're carved from the same beast. As an animal has different ribs, each rib is from the animal. So it is with this spiritual beast. Although Marxism, socialism, and communism may be presented as different and have various sects, they're from the same beast. They have the same end result. I'll use Marxism to mean the whole belief system.

Volumes have been written about Marxism. And the acceptance of Marxism has been a worldwide phenomenon. Marxism excludes any existence of God with its foundation based on evolution. There is no place in the Christian life for this godless belief. Deception is the only outcome of those who follow Marxist theories.

The Marxist theory is based on the assertion that (1) mankind's progress through history is a scientific process without the involvement of God, sin, the devil, or the fall of mankind and (2) materialist philosophy. This philosophy is called dialectical materialism. Essentially, the theory describes life evolving around the production of materials and goods. Each stage of the evolution (epoch) is a struggle between classes of people. Each epoch has a dominate class (a thesis) that controls the means of production. The thesis is also in charge of the wealth, which is distributed unequally. The fallen nature of man, the influence of a personal devil, or the divine intervention of God is not to be ascribed to. Mankind is to evolve into a being that will obliterate greed, crime, and sin from society and advance into a purist communist society.

The nondominant class is the worker who must labor for sustenance and survival. He works for the thesis. The workers are the antithesis. When the antithesis influences or overcomes the thesis, a new social class (synthesis) is born. The synthesis becomes the new thesis, and the process begins again.

According to this belief system, the history of mankind evolves in this fashion:

1. **Primitive Communal Society**: During this period, there was no structured society, and all means of production belonged to the people. However, because there was no means of protection, the weak were overcome by stronger elements that oppressed the weak and secured for themselves the means of production, thereby creating a new society.

2. **Ancient Slave-Holding Society**: During this epoch wealthy landowners (the thesis) forced slaves to produce for them. Overlords shared in the profits, and the slaves were given a paltry subsistence. The oppressed became the antithesis and revolted. Eventually, the ancient slave-holding society evolved into the next epoch stage.

3. **Feudalism**: In the feudalist period, landowners (landlords) distributed some of their land for lease to the serfs who worked the land, shared the produce, and provided military service. The peasants (slaves, serfs, and freemen) became the antithesis. Numerous clashes occurred, and eventually, a new society evolved; especially as industrialization progressed.

4. **Capitalism**: Capitalism is large amounts of wealth horded in the coffers of individuals and businesses. This great wealth created the new ruling class, the bourgeoisie, who use their wealth to wield power and influence over the state and governments. The working class, the proletariat, opposed the bourgeoisie. The bourgeoisie owns the means

of production and pays the working class a meager wage. Furthermore, because of their great wealth and influence, they force smaller companies out of business. These former owners become part of the proletariat. As the proletariat grows, the capitalist class subsides. Production increases, and a surplus is produced, resulting in unemployment, diminished production, and depression. The proletariat revolt, overthrow the capitalist system, and create a new synthesis.

5. **Socialism**: Socialism is based on *scientific theories* that turns all production over to the state and abolishes all private ownership. The transition between capitalism and socialism is the transition of privately owned production to the ownership and control of all production by the state. Because the capitalist will not voluntarily give control of private property and production to the socialist, force and deception are sanctioned, and a dictatorship of the proletariat is to be established. This system is to be led by the communist vanguard. The term communist vanguard is best defined by the Marxist themselves.

In any social movement there is a vanguard and a mass; these two concepts are meaningless outside of the movement of which they are integral parts, mutually constituted by their relation in development of the movement. The vanguard are groups of people who are more resolute and committed, better organized and able to take a leading role in the struggle, and on the other side, the <u>mass</u>, are larger numbers of people who participate in the struggle or are involved simply by their social position, but are less committed or well-placed in relation to the struggle, and will participate only in the decisive moment, which in fact change history. There is a continual movement and exchange between vanguard and mass.

The Marxist theory of the vanguard, in relation to *class struggle* under capitalism, holds that the working class (the mass) needs to be militantly lead through revolutionary struggle against capitalism and in the building of Socialism. The communist vanguard is made up of those who are in the forefront of workers' struggle, engaged in struggles against the capitalist state and the management of the firms which are "branches" of the ruling class. (www.marxists.org/glossary/terms/v/a.htm)

The vanguard is to destroy the opposition and reeducate the people to their responsibilities as members of a socialist society. In essence, socialism is the cleansing system used to obliterate all opposition to the utopian system of communism.

6. **Communism**: Communism, as believed by the Marxists, is the highest and purist social system. It's the total absolution of private property, and all means of production then belong to the people. Everyone is to share equally in the profits, and government is abolished. (Think John Lennon's song "Imagine".) Communism cannot exist unless everyone is willing to do exactly as required. Hence, the purging process by the communist vanguard (the progressive movement in the United States). There cannot be any opposition. Any opposition must be abolished by whatever the state deems appropriate. There is no divine command of right and wrong. It is the state that ultimately decides morality.

There is no God in the Marxist faith except man. The murder and persecution of the masses is justified in order to purge society from all opposition, real or imagined. Then people can create the purist social system—communism. In reality, there has never been a true communist system. What we can see are nations such as the PRC and the former USSR as communist vanguards. They forced the masses into an ideology though fear, intimidation, murder, and educational deception. The influence of Marxism can be easily seen throughout the earth, and the United States is no exception.

This beast has indeed devoured much flesh.

The Third Beast

Daniel 7:6 says, "After this I beheld, and lo another, like a leopard, which had upon the back of it four wings of a fowl; the beast had also four heads; and dominion was given to it."

Leopards are spotted carnivores, very swift and powerful. They're hunters. I think it's no mistake that God used a leopard for this beast. The leopard is a spotted beast that blends into its hunting grounds and is ready to pounce upon unsuspecting prey. When I consider this beast, I think of the United Nations. The United Nations is a spotted organization that blends into the nations it inhabits. It is always ready to introduce its own agendas into the fabric of its prey until that quarry becomes digested into the beast. In other words, through political influence or deception this beast will introduce program after program into a nation until that nation has lost its national identity and succumbs to its doctrine. It's the leader of the one-world movement.

This beast has four wings. It is swift and has the ability to go anywhere in its domain at incredible speeds. It has four heads. It is an organization that no one authority has control over. It is a beast to which dominion is given. It has no authority on its own. The nations that are a part of it give it power and dominion. Its allegiance is to itself, but its ties are strongly Marxist. Freedom, liberty, nationalism, self-reliance, self-sufficiency, and individuality are the natural enemies of this beast.

It's a strong beast. After all, the support of multiple nations (in particular the United States) gives it wealth and military power. Perhaps its greatest weakness is its politically correct worldview.

Such a worldview seems to have no common sense. It short-circuits its own power and prosperity, and thus, it cannot see the danger of or effectively stand against the fourth beast.

The Fourth Beast

Daniel 7:7–8 says,

> After this I saw in the night visions, and behold a fourth beast, dreadful and terrible, and strong exceedingly; and it had great iron teeth: it devoured and brake in pieces, and stamped the residue with the feet of it: and it was diverse from all the beasts that were before it; and it had ten horns. I considered the horns, and, behold, there came up among them another little horn, before whom there were three of the first horns plucked up by the roots: and, behold, in this horn were eyes like the eyes of man, and a mouth speaking great things.

Daniel 7:23–25 says,

> Thus he said, The fourth beast shall be the fourth kingdom upon earth, which shall be diverse from all kingdoms, and shall devour the whole earth, and shall tread it down, and break it in pieces. And the ten horns out of this kingdom are ten kings that shall arise: and another shall rise after them; and he shall be diverse from the first, and he shall subdue three kings. And he shall speak great words against the most High, and shall wear out the saints of the most High, and think to change times and laws: and they shall be given into his hand until a time and times and the dividing of time.

This fourth beast is violent, destructive, and powerful (dreadful, terrible, and exceedingly strong). It devours (conquers), breaks in pieces (divides people and nations), and tramples the residue (murders, terrorizes, and manipulates). This beast isn't a nation because it has ten horns (ten rulers or powers) that control it. Nonetheless, the horns have the same motivating desires and beliefs, and they are working toward world domination.

I see Islam in this beast. It is dreadful, terrible, and exceedingly strong. It conquers, divides people and nations, murders, terrorizes, and manipulates whomever it does not conquer or destroy.

From the beast that was "devouring, breaking in pieces, and trampling the residue with its feet" comes a horn. This is reminiscent of our opening text. Daniel 9:26–27 says,

> And after threescore and two weeks shall Messiah be cut off, but not for himself: and the people of the prince that shall come shall destroy the city and the sanctuary; and the end thereof shall be with a flood, and unto the end of the war desolations are determined. And he shall confirm the covenant with many for one week: and in the midst of the week he shall cause the sacrifice and the oblation to cease, and for the overspreading of abominations he shall make it desolate, even until the consummation, and that determined shall be poured upon the desolate.

Consider the similarities:

1. A beast arises that conquers, divides, and terrorizes.
2. The people of the prince who is to come (the Beast) shall destroy the city and the sanctuary and brings a war of desolation.

3. Out of the beast arises another figure that takes control of the beast and brings persecution against the saints and intends to change times and laws to fit his agenda.
4. The prince who is to come takes control of the people who destroy the city and the sanctuary. This prince brings desolation.

Now here's where our texts come together. This beast represents the "people of the prince that shall come." The people are bringing war, destruction, and desolation. And then another horn takes control over the beast. He causes a world peace by covenant for one week (or seven years). The earth is quiet for three and a half years, but "in the middle of the week he shall bring an end to sacrifice and offering. And on the wings of abominations shall be one who makes desolate (NKJV)." He shall break the covenant and set himself up as earth's supreme ruler and set about to destroy saints of the Most High.

Daniel 7:8, 24 (NKJV) says,

> I was considering the horns, and there was another horn, a little one, coming up among them, before whom three of the first horns were plucked out by the roots. And there, in this horn, were eyes like the eyes of a man, and a mouth speaking pompous words … The ten horns are ten kings who shall arise from this kingdom. And another shall rise **after** them; he shall be different from first ones, and shall subdue three kings. He shall speak pompous words against the Most High, shall persecute the saints of the Most High, and shall intend to change times and law. Then the saints shall be given into his hand for a time and times and a half a time. But the court shall be seated, and they shall take away his dominion, to consume and destroy it forever. (emphasis mine)

In 2 Thessalonians 2:3–5, Paul says this about him: "Let no man deceive you by any means: for that day shall not come, except there come a falling away first, and that man of sin be revealed, the son of perdition; Who opposeth and exalteth himself above all that is called God, or that is worshipped; so that he as God sitteth in the temple of God, shewing himself that he is God. Remember ye not, that, when I was yet with you, I told you these things?"

The book of Revelation describes the Beast in Revelation 13:1– 10, which says

> And I stood upon the sand of the sea, and saw a beast rise up out of the sea, having seven heads and ten horns, and upon his horns ten crowns, and upon his heads the name of blasphemy. And the beast which I saw was like unto a leopard, and his feet were as the feet of a bear, and his mouth as the mouth of a lion: and the dragon gave him his power, and his seat, and great authority. And I saw one of his heads as it were wounded to death; and his deadly wound was healed: and all the world wondered after the beast. And they worshipped the dragon which gave power unto the beast: and they worshipped the beast, saying, Who is like unto the beast? who is able to make war with him?
>
> And there was given unto him a mouth speaking great things and blasphemies; and power was given unto him to continue forty and two months. And he opened his mouth in blasphemy against God, to blaspheme his name, and his tabernacle, and them that dwell in heaven. And it was given unto him to make war with the saints, and to overcome them: and power was given him over all kindreds, and tongues, and nations. And all that dwell upon the earth shall worship him,

> whose names are not written in the book of life of the Lamb slain from the foundation of the world.
>
> If any man have an ear, let him hear. He that leadeth into captivity shall go into captivity: he that killeth with the sword must be killed with the sword. Here is the patience and the faith of the saints.

John describes the beast as a conglomerate of all four beasts found in Daniel. This beast is like a leopard. His feet are like a bear. His mouth is like a lion, and it has ten horns. It's as though the fourth beast gains control and influence over the other beasts. Then the other beasts throw in their power with the Antichrist. In fact, the whole world marvels and follows the beast. And authority over every tribe, tongue, and nation was given him. Where does he get this authority? From the other beasts. Of course, Satan is behind this. If you think about it, Satan offered Jesus the kingdoms of the world as a temptation. Matthew 4:8–11 says, "Again, the devil taketh him up into an exceeding high mountain, and sheweth him all the kingdoms of the world, and the glory of them; And saith unto him, All these things will I give thee, if thou wilt fall down and worship me. Then saith Jesus unto him, Get thee hence, Satan: for it is written, Thou shalt worship the Lord thy God, and him only shalt thou serve. Then the devil leaveth him, and, behold, angels came and ministered unto him."

For this lesson, my point is that the fourth beast shall bring destruction and chaos in the last of the last days. The confusion and deception that the other beasts have caused in the earth amplifies the influence and destruction of the fourth beast. This chaos will principally come from a *beast* that is fielded by ten authorities with the same objectives and motivations. During this time, another shall come on the scene and cause peace where there was none. The world will come to rely on this individual. This individual that controls the *beast* is the one we call the Antichrist. He is the one to whom Satan delegates his power. He will cause the world to follow him and hate and persecute the saints for three and a half years. But in the end, eternal damnation will be his reward, and the saints shall inherit the everlasting kingdom.

Conclusion

It has been my endeavor to present to you the scriptural evidence for an accurate chronological order of the end times. It appears to me that many of God's loving children are ill equipped or prepared for the realities of the last of the last days. US Army Special Forces have a guideline that says, "Proper prior planning prevents pitiful poor performance." If the child of God has an escape mentality, proper spiritual growth or mental maturity may not occur. Being unprepared gives place to the devil. Remember Peter's exhortation to "be sober, be vigilant; because your adversary the devil walks about like a roaring lion, seeking whom he may devour" (1 Peter 5:8). Heed that warning. Every quality soldier takes preparation seriously. He will know the enemy's behavior, and he will be proficient with his own tactics and weaponry. He lives by the adage, "More sweat in training is less blood in combat." So is the serious soldier of the Lord.

God is calling His people into the battle for souls, especially for the souls of your loved ones. No parent, child, or friend who is sober and thinking rationally would be so concerned with the things of this world that they neglect their part in seeing their loved ones enter eternity with Jesus. We need to practice the love of God, learn how to pray according to the word of God, and be available to minister the gospel to the lost. Eternity is forever, and you could be cut off from the presence of God.

My heart and desire for you is found in Colossians 1:9–11, which says, "Father, I pray for the readers of this work. I desire and ask that they my be filled with the knowledge of your will in all wisdom and spiritual understanding; that they may walk worthy of the Lord, fully pleasing him, being fruitful in every good work and increasing in the knowledge of God; strengthened with all might, according to your glorious power, for all patience and longsuffering with joy."

In Jesus's name, amen.

Prayer for Salvation

God's not a religion. He's a person. He loves you. He desires a relationship with you, specifically a father-child relationship. Jesus came to make that possible in a very personal way. You can know where you will spend eternity! When you make Jesus your Lord and Savior, "the Spirit itself beareth witness with our spirit, that we are the children of God" (Romans 8:16). God didn't make it difficult to become His child. Jesus made it possible. Jesus took your sins and shortcomings on the cross. "Who his own self bare our sins in his own body on the tree, that we, being dead to sins, should live unto righteousness: by whose stripes ye were healed" (1 Peter 2:24).

Romans 10:9 explains how simple it is to enter into God's kingdom. "That if thou shalt confess with thy mouth the Lord Jesus, and shalt believe in thine heart that God hath raised him from the dead, thou shalt be saved."

When you declare Jesus as your Lord, you're literally changing spiritual kingdoms. It's akin to swearing allegiance to the United States upon becoming a new citizen. Not only does the kingdom of God become your new eternal home, but you become God's child as well "As newborn babes, desire the sincere milk of the word, that ye may grow thereby" (1 Peter 2:2). Please pray this prayer so that you may receive the life that God has for you.

Father God, You said that if I will confess Jesus as my Lord and believe in my heart that You raised Him from the dead, I would be saved. I do that now.

Jesus, I confess You as my Lord, and I believe that God has raised You from the dead.

Father, I thank You for this eternal contract of Your promise. I thank You for loving me and saving me. Please teach me Your word so that I may grow to know You better and in a more personal way. Thank You for Your love. I love and appreciate you.

In Jesus's name, amen.

APPENDIX

Book of Revelation Timeline

This timeline is designed to give the reader a quick overview of the book of Revelation events and their respective order and interaction.

Messages to the Churches: Given for instruction and correction, these messages are valid for all Christians throughout the Church age.

Seals and Trumpets

First Seal: The Abomination of Desolation.
Second Seal: War.
Third Seal: Famine and Recession.
Fourth Seal: Death by crime, beasts, and hunger.
Fifth Seal: Martyred souls cry out for justice.
Sixth Seal: Sun darkened. Moon not giving its light. Stars fall from heaven, and the powers of the heavens will be shaken (Matthew 24:29; Mark 13:24–25; Luke 21:25–26). Take note that after this event, Jesus states, "Then they will see the Son of Man coming," but doesn't specify a time period.
Seventh Seal: The seven trumpets begin to sound (1 Corinthians 15:51–53) At the last trumpet, Jesus gathers us to Himself.

- First, hail and fire mingles with blood. A third of the trees and all green grass are burned up.
- Second, a mountain of fire is thrown into the sea. A third of the see becomes blood, a third of the living creatures in the sea die, and a third of the ships are destroyed.
- Third, wormwood star falls, and a third of rivers and springs become bitter.
- Fourth, a third of the sun and moon darkened, and a third of the stars in the sky become black too.
- Fifth (first woe), the bottomless pit is opened. Demons have the power to hurt people for five months.
- Sixth, the angels at the Euphrates are released and gather a two-hundred-million-strong army.
  - Little book that, when eaten, is sweet in the mouth but bitter in the stomach (Could this refer to "the days of vengeance" found in Luke 21:22?)
  - Gentiles trample the holy city for forty-two months. (This is the same amount of time that the Antichrist "as God sitteth in the temple of God." 2 Thess. 2:4)
  - The two witnesses prophesy for 1,260 days.
  - (I think that the Spirit is letting us know that there are two witnesses and informing us of how long their ministry is—not that their ministry starts with the sounding of the sixth trumpet. The Antichrist rules for forty-two months(appx. 1,260 days), yet reading this passage the seventh trumpet is about to sound. I believe that the resurrection of the two witnesses occurs simultaneously with the *rapture*.
- Seventh, Jesus gathers His people (rapture).

Bowls of Wrath

First: Loathsome sores are on all those who worship and receive the mark, name, or number of the Beast.

Second: The sea turns to blood.

Third: The rivers and springs turn to blood.

Fourth: Scorching heat plague those of the earth.

Fifth: Kingdom of the Beast is filled with darkness and people gnaw their tongues because of pain.

Sixth: The Euphrates River is dried up.

Seventh: The greatest earthquake occurs since men have been on the earth, Babylon's evil is remembered, every mountain and island flee, and a great hailstorm happens.

Doom of Babylon

Jesus Returns as King of Kings to Reign for a Millennium

- Armageddon
  - The Beast and false prophet cast alive into the lake of fire.
  - The rest of the army is killed.
- Satan is bound.
- Saints rule with Jesus.
- Satan is released after a thousand years, when he then deceives the nations to war on Jesus and the saints.
- We encounter the great white throne judgment and the destruction of the old heaven and earth.

Finally, we will experience the new heaven and earth in eternity.

Bowls of Wrath Outline

This outline is prepared so the reader can easily view what God refers to as His wrath. Many plagues occur during the great tribulation, and life on the planet will be stressful. But the worst of the plagues come when God pours out His wrath.

1. First Bowl (Revelation 16:1)
   a. This bowl is poured on the earth.
   b. A foul and loathsome sore upon those who have the mark of the Beast and those who worship his image.
2. Second Bowl (Revelation 16:3)
   a. This is poured on the sea.
   b. The sea becomes as blood.
   c. Every creature in the sea dies.
3. Third Bowl (Revelation 16:4–7)
   a. This is poured on the rivers and springs.
   b. They become as blood.
4. Fourth Bowl (Revelation 16:8–9)
   a. This is poured on sun.
   b. People are with scorched with great heat.
5. Fifth Bowl (Revelation 16:10–11)
   a. This poured on the throne of the Beast.
   b. His kingdom is filled with darkness.
   c. Those in the Beast's kingdom gnaw their tongues because of pain and sores.

6. Sixth Bowl (Revelation 16:12–16)
   a. This is poured on the Euphrates River.
   b. The river is dried up.
   c. Spirits come out of the mouths of the dragon, beast, and false prophet to perform signs and gather the people to Armageddon.
7. Seventh Bowl (Revelation 16:17–21)
   a. This is poured into the air.
   b. There are noises, thunder, and lighting.
   c. There is a great earthquake. The great city is divided into three parts, and the cities of the nations fall.
   d. Every island flees away and the mountains are not found.
   e. Seventy-five-pound hail falls.
   f. Babylon is remembered.

Armageddon to the Millennial Reign Timeline

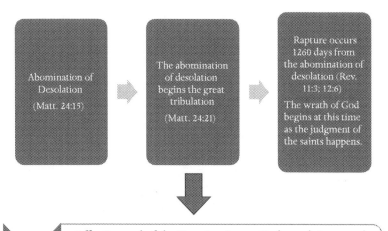

Abomination of Desolation (Matt. 24:15)

The abomination of desolation begins the great tribulation (Matt. 24:21)

Rapture occurs 1260 days from the abomination of desolation (Rev. 11:3; 12:6)

The wrath of God begins at this time as the judgment of the saints happens.

1290 Days Dan. 12:11

- Effective end of the Beast's reign as God wrath is poured out.
- The Beast prepares his armies for Armageddon.

Return of the King

- 1335 days (Daniel 12:12) to the return of the king and Armageddon.

Millenial Reign Rev. 20:1 -10

- Christ's thousand -year reign.
- Satan is let loose after a thousand years.

Time Link Chart for the End Times

Time, Times, and Half a Time	2,300 Days	42 Months	1,290 Days	1,260 Days
1. Dan. 7:25 2. Dan. 12:7 3. Rev. 12:14	1. Dan. 8:14	1. Rev. 13:5 2. Rev. 11:2	1. Dan. 12:11	1. Rev. 11:3 2. Rev. 12:6
1. Saints given into his hand.	1. From daily sacrifices and Transgression of Desolation	1. Beast to continue.	1. Daily sacrifice taken away & Abomination of Desolation.	1. Two witnesses.
2. Fulfillment of all these things.		2. Holy city tread.		2. Woman in the wilderness.
3. Woman in the wilderness.				

1,335 Days	Five Months
1. Dan. 12:12	1. Rev. 9:10
1. Blessed is he who comes to this time.	1. Fifth trumpet 2. Locust hurt men.

Pretribulation Process

Daniel 9:26–27 (NKJV) says, "And the people of the prince who is to come shall destroy the city and the sanctuary. The end of it shall be with a flood, and till the end of the war desolations are determined. Then_he shall confirm a covenant with many for one week; but in the middle of the week he shall bring an end to sacrifice and offering. And on the wing of abominations shall be one who makes desolate, even until the consummation, which is determined, is poured out on the desolate. (emphasis mine)

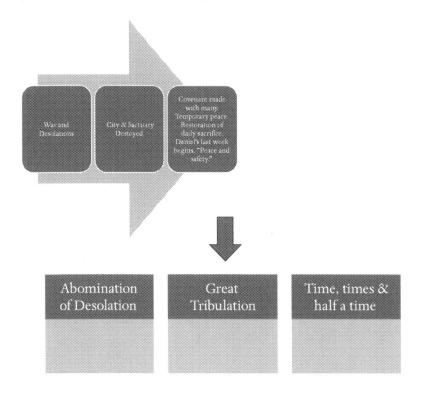

Covenant is broken after three and a half years.

Printed in the United States
By Bookmasters